SAVING
CHURCH

SAVING CHURCH

Restoring the People of God
with Missional Evangelism

MARTYN ATKINS
AND
KEN CARTER

invite
PRESS

Plano, Texas

CONTENTS

Part Two: The Mission-Shaped Church

Introduction

This book is intended for small groups and individuals, both lay and ordained, who are interested in and convicted by God's Holy Spirit about their churches becoming more "mission-shaped", committed to a new kind of evangelism, and creating healthy "fresh expressions" of church. It contains reflections on Bible passages, teaching about evangelism and mission, shared stories, observations, examples, and suggestions about how our churches can become more available and useful to the Holy Spirit, wherever they may be planted. Within these chapters, you will find stopping points along the way for pauses, prayer, conversations, silence, and sharing.

The book is written by two experienced senior Methodist pastors. They are leaders and friends, one American and one British—both deeply committed to what they write about. Their input and insights come from both sides of the Atlantic and will hopefully enrich and benefit congregations in both the United States and the United Kingdom alike. Both authors have been privileged to travel much of the world learning and speaking about mission, evangelism, and fresh expressions of church, so you will also find a world church flavor to this book.

We draw deeply from tradition while recognizing the need for evolution and renewal. Because we are Methodists, we have included references to John and Charles Wesley, the Methodist, Wesleyan tradition, and its emphases and idiosyncrasies. However, this book is not intended solely for Methodist Christians, and we hope that in these increasingly post-denominational times, Christians of many parts of the One Church of Jesus Christ will benefit from its lessons.

In recent years, many resources about fresh expressions, evangelism, and mission-shaped church have been produced, including some by the authors of this one! Today, some congregations are already well along the way to reshaping and reimagining their churches, and we rejoice in that. Others are wary of all talk of fresh expressions and evangelism. This book speaks to both these groups but is primarily offered as an encouraging and challenging primer for those still thousands of local churches that know little about mission-shaped thinking or practice or fresh expressions of church and are possibly ambivalent about evangelism but realize increasingly that ignorance is not bliss and continuing commitment to Christ requires greater openness and holy risk-taking. We have confidence in the good news of Jesus Christ and a humility about what we have learned, are still learning, and what we have to share. Thank you for being on this journey with us. If it stimulates, irritates, inspires, challenges, informs, and transforms, then we rejoice!

Narrative Glossary

Meanings and Longings

For those quite new to terms like mission-shaped church, inherited church, mixed economy, blended ecology, and fresh expressions, an initial brief explanation will probably help.

Mission-Shaped churches actively desire to be configured primarily by mission—what they sense God wants them to be and do, and where and with whom God sends them. As we shall explore shortly, the ministry and commission of Jesus, together with the realization that God is a God of mission and on mission, both give shape and direction to being a "mission-shaped church." They are essentially outward facing and focused on being with and among others who don't yet believe or belong to Christ. They are increasingly aware that this involves more than simply seeking to be attractive or invitational. Such churches are aided, informed, and *reshaped* by the evolving insights about good mission theology and practices, and fertile ways of being church today, to which they themselves contribute. We use the term *mission-shaped church* to describe such churches.

Inherited Church is a common way of describing in deliberately non-judgmental terms, a model of church that has been numerically and culturally dominant almost everywhere for a very long time. Dedicated buildings. Established congregations. Sunday worship. Paid pastor or priest and sometimes other workers. Committees and offerings. Two brief points must be made here. First, in every historic denomination, this model of church remains dominant and normative, a physical and organizational symbol of past commitment and effectiveness, and present durability. A precious gift passed on to us by the saints of past generations; a valuable inheritance we must learn to steward well without creating mere museums or heritage sites. Second, the severe decline in churchgoing in most first-world contexts and increasingly other areas of the globe, inevitably begs questions about inherited churches, which (though there are always exceptions) are, taken overall, clearly failing to attract, convert and disciple increasing numbers of contemporary human beings. Thus, the increasingly urgent need for new forms of church. We use the term *inherited church* to identify such churches.

A third point needs to be made here because it's vitally important. Inherited churches can and do become more mission-shaped without necessarily ceasing to be inherited churches by type. Nevertheless, there's always a *reshaping* involved. A vital reshaping is a change of heart and mind, a *metanoia* (Mark 1: 15) about *ownership* and *purpose*. An increasing realization that the church isn't ours but God's, so our primary calling isn't to look after it for God but rather repeatedly hand it and ourselves to God. With the costly consequence for many a long-standing settled church congregation that what *God* wants us to be like becomes progressively more important and transformative than what *we* want to be like. Leading to a congregation making crucial decisions: are we going to change and try to live (and perhaps die trying) or hunker down, almost always decline, and finally die?

Diversity is at the heart of the notion of *mixed economies and mixed or blended ecologies of church and fresh expressions.* The phrase *mixed economy* was used by Rowan Williams to describe his hoped-for future landscape of church. This has become common currency to indicate that just as most economies include a mixture of elements (private, public, regulatory, and so on) so in respect of "church," a diversity of forms co-existing in relationships of mutual respect, support, and encouragement is needed, desired, and worked for. More recently the phrase *mixed ecology of church* with its allusions to varied healthy species rather than units of production is preferred by many. But whether *economy/ecology*, the basic point is the same. Church today needs to be varied and diverse not multiples of much the same thing. More recently still, Michael Beck in his book

Deep and Wild describes how, over time, a natural outcome of different forms of church existing in symbiotic relationship is a blending that creates nascent forms of church. This he terms blended ecology which, like blended families and cultures brings into being non-identical reproductions of its nature and form. In other words, we are only at the beginning of witnessing fresh expressions of church.

It's important to note that when we talk about diversity of church we're not talking about diversity in terms of different Church *denominations*—we've got that aplenty already. Rather we mean diversity of *expressions, types* and *models*, the fruits of a blended ecology. Ideally, a diversity of expressions of church is needed in every locality, and *every* church needs to be the *best* expression of its type it can be. The life of *all* church congregations needs to relate to and mirror the heights and depths of human experiences. Their caring and serving needs to be excellent. They must be hospitable and attractive, Christ-bearing and deeply contextual. They need to be profoundly mission minded. In short, the mixed economy or ecology isn't a collection of the drab, the sad, and the bad. It's a healthy diversity of good church. More fundamentally, this reality is grounded in the diverse spiritual gifts that bless the One Body of Christ (I Corinthians 12-14). This is increasingly required as it appears that there's no happy future for inherited church *done badly*. Such churches seem increasingly unable to attract and reach hardly anybody other than the faithful souls who already belong to them.

Despite this harsh reality however, the mixed economy/ecology is conveniently misconstrued by some to mean "we'll just stay as we are and those who want to do new things can do them." Another version of this (sometimes deliberate) misunderstanding is ecumenical in nature, suggesting that Catholics continue to do their thing, and Methodists do theirs, and new church groupings do new things, and everyone is happy! But everyone isn't happy. Many denominational leaders, movers, and shakers all recognize the need to create a more diverse economy/ecology of church in their own traditions. They know more than most that sustaining old, tired denominational identities is not the blended church eco system which is so critically needed. We use the term *mixed economy/ecology* to indicate this kind of diversity of church *type*.

In recent years the phrase *fresh expressions* has been increasingly questioned, at least in the United Kingdom. Isn't it old hat, a bit twee and quaint? Haven't we moved on from such phrases? Perhaps, though in many parts of the United States and the world it remains exciting and vital. We continue to use the phrase as it helpfully includes a wide variety of experiments and initiatives, models and types. As such, it remains a good catch-all term for the vitality and variety emerging in so many places today.

A subtle difference between mission-shaped church and fresh expressions can now be discerned. Almost all fresh expressions seek (indeed, are created) to be mission-shaped, but not all mission-shaped churches are necessarily fresh expressions. An overriding purpose of this book is to urge all church congregations to become as mission-shaped as possible (which, we believe, necessarily involves appropriate, reimagined evangelism); blossoming as a rich and diverse blended ecology of church; and involving the proliferation of fresh expressions in each denomination, area, and congregation.

Pause...

Share together what has been most helpful and most alarming about the brief descriptions of mission-shaped and inherited church.

Another way of articulating this is to outline the nature of the church we pray for, long for, work for, and seek:

1. *Grounded in Scripture.* The church we are seeking 'reads and hears' scripture every day. It expects to hear a fresh word from God, one that corrects and comforts—one that guides and heals. It is open to be changed by that word.

2. *An Evangelical Heart.* The church we are seeking understands the importance of transformation of life, a change that happens at the cross, where sins are forgiven, new life begins, and Christlikeness takes shape.

3. *Non-Judgmental.* The church we are seeking restrains itself from judging the flaws and imperfections of others, knowing that only God is in a position to condemn. It knows it has enough problems of its own to work on anyway.

4. *More Communal than Individual.* The church we are seeking remembers that the Old Testament is the story of a people, not an individual, and the New Testament is written for and to churches. Salvation is essentially incorporation into the Body of Christ.

5. *A Passion for Justice.* The church we are seeking remembers that God hears the cries of the oppressed and that God is always on the side of the poor, the marginalized and the forgotten. God's people likewise prioritize these things with passion and in a way that crosses and transcends politically partisan lines.

6. *A Movement Into the World.* The church we are seeking knows it exists not for itself, but for the God of mission and the mission of God in the world. It recognizes that in order to discover our true reason for being, we must loose hold on other, lesser reasons for being, holding fast to the promise that Jesus will be with us outside the walls of his church.

7. *The Glory and Beauty of the Lord.* The church we are seeking often finds itself lost in wonder, love and praise, standing amazed in the presence of an awesome God who is both infinitely powerful and gloriously near in the present moment.

Whether newly planted or well established, traditional, inherited, or fresh, we believe such a church is potent as an evangelistic mission-shaped community sent into God's world today, resourced and accompanied by the Spirit of God.

Pause...

Talk through the list of seven characteristics of 'the church we pray for, long for, work for, and seek.' Which are most important to you? Which are well formed in your local church, and which need to become more developed?

Do you want to add any further characteristics to your list?

PART ONE

Biblical Reflections

The first few chapters contain reflections and comments on passages from the Gospels and the Acts of the Apostles. We pay particular attention to themes and learning that we believe enable churches to become more mission-shaped and fertile with fresh expressions and reimagined evangelism. Taken together, they also offer us a deeper understanding of both the *Great Commission* and the *missio Dei*, concepts that we will explain along the way. We've added stopping points throughout and questions for those wishing to delve a bit deeper.

Gracious God, Open your holy Word to our lives, hearts, and churches.
Open our lives, hearts, and churches to your holy Word. Amen.

Matthew's Great Commission

We begin by reflecting on the Great Commission in Matthew 28:18-20, a passage that rightly remains a key mission text for very many Christians and churches today.

Jesus came and said to them, "All authority in heaven and on earth has been given to me. Go therefore and make disciples of all nations, baptizing them in the name of the Father and of the Son and of the Holy Spirit, and teaching them to obey everything that I have commanded you. And remember, I am with you always, to the end of the age."

Today, almost all biblically literate people know the phrase "The Great Commission" and the passage of scripture to which it refers. But it wasn't always so. Not until the late seventeenth century did this passage in Matthew slowly begin to be known in this way. Prior to this, it was generally thought that this commission of Jesus was given only to the eleven disciples who first heard it. It was regarded as providing the impetus for the dynamic kick-start to the spread of Christianity recorded in the book of Acts, fueled by the coming of the Holy Spirit upon the disciples at Pentecost. So, at least by implied logic, when the last apostle died, the apostolic commission died with it, by which time the Christian fire was well and truly lit. Put simply, the Great Commission was for the special few rather than the ordinary many.

By the mid-eighteenth century, John Wesley was among the earlier adopters to preach on this passage as a command of Jesus to all believers, though he tended to expound Christ's commission from the text itself rather than refer explicitly to Matthew 28:18-20 as the *Great*

Commission. Since that time, until recent decades, the commission Jesus gave to the disciples in the last verses of Matthew's Gospel has virtually become synonymous with the nature and purpose of Christian mission.

> All authority is given
> to me. . . . Go therefore . . .

The *therefore* is important. The command to go is consequent on Jesus' *authority.* Jesus has authority over heaven and earth because He is the Living One who died and has risen from the dead. His resurrection makes clear that he is who he said he was, and his teachings are true. Therefore, the disciples can believe and have confidence in him. This enables and shapes the message they're commissioned to make known.

We see several resurrection appearances of Jesus recorded in the Gospels, mostly in John and Luke. Matthew's account of the resurrection and what occurs afterwards is straightforward. The two Marys go to the tomb and are met by an angel who tells them that Jesus is risen. They must tell his disciples this great news and that he will meet them in Galilee. Then, Jesus himself appears to the women and reiterates the message of the angel. We can assume that's what the women did, as the next we read of the (male) disciples, they "went to Galilee, to the mountain where Jesus had told them to go" (28:16). Jesus' appearance there is the first and only time he appears to the (male) disciples. Consequently, the words we now call the Great Commission are the only instructions recorded in Matthew that the risen Jesus gives to them. We have no exchanges with frightened disciples locked away in a room as in John, no long conversations while journeying to Emmaus as in Luke, and no forty days speaking of the kingdom of God as in Acts. We have in Matthew only these words, spoken on the mountain.

We're meant to note that Jesus is on a mountain when he gives this commission. Matthew has a thing about mountains. When you go up a mountain, God is going to declare something wonderful. It is Matthew who collects key teachings of Jesus in what we call the sermon on the mount, Matthew who expands Mark's story of Jesus' transfiguration on a "high mountain", and who alone tells us that Jesus' face is shining like the sun, just as Moses' face shone after he'd talked with God on another mountain. This connection with Moses is significant. God gave the Law—the quintessential instructions for life—from a mountain and delivered it through Moses to the people of God. Here, on a mountain, more vital instructions are given to believers by one who is the Son of God.

Go.

The command is to *go*, though actually no *going* is recorded in Matthew. The Gospel ends with the disciples on the mountain, Jesus' words of commission and assurance ringing in their ears. The book of Acts, however, records much *going*, and we will reflect on some key mission passages from Acts later.

Nowadays, many of our churches spend most of their time and effort inviting people to come rather than *going* anywhere much at all. They seem to be instinctively *Temple* rather than *Ark (of the Covenant)* shaped. It's more of a waiting-for than a walking-to approach. During a time when sufficient numbers of people found us, inviting people to come worked well. Enough numbers joined, and we could be (perhaps) excused for thinking that *going* wasn't really necessary. We could make a decent case for immobility. Clearly at some point in the past, someone did obey the command to *go*; otherwise, our church would never have been founded, but we tend to believe now that the *going* job is done. We have been here long enough for folks to know where we are, what we say, and that if they want to come and join us, they will be welcome. Our job now is to keep our church (by which we mean this building) going, without really *going* anywhere else. Many readers will note the problem, however. This kind of narrative has persisted long after its sell-by date. In increasing numbers of local churches, the sobering reality is that inviting people to come has become less and less effective, and the problem is not solved by shouting the invitation louder or trying to make things more attractive and comfortable for those who happen along.

One of the most common features of mission-shaped churches, especially inherited churches in transition to greater mission-shapedness, and most certainly a key feature of fresh expressions, is that they *move*. A long-established church starts to plant new communities among different people groups or areas, whether congregations or small groups, whether in homes, public spaces, or empty church buildings. Or a group of Christians is sent to serve and gather for worship and often to *move* to live and work in a new vicinity. Importantly, the aim is not to replicate existing churches but to offer a fresh expression of that church that can reach new people with God's love in Christ. The *going* may mean that the church remains geographically located where it is, but it *moves* to become a different sort of place and community, turned outwards toward others, reshaped for God's mission. *Going* isn't simply about overseas mission or donating generously to multiple good causes, though that is a good, neccessary thing to do. Rather, *going* is the call of God to every local church, however currently set and sedentary, to *move* into new places and spaces among those who have no living, contemporary experience of Christ and His people.

In the former central offices of the British Methodist Church in London was the Richmond Room, a large room named after Richmond College, the place where those accepted by the (Wesleyan) Methodist Missionary Society (MMS) were trained for overseas mission service. The college closed in the early 1970s, and its library and artefacts were distributed to various places. Its memorial boards went to Methodist Church House. Several very large gilt lettered wooden boards were each dedicated to a country or part of the world to which the MMS sent missionaries, including West Africa, South Africa, Malaya, Pacific Islands. Some of the missionaries who were sent there are listed with the year they entered the college and the year they died.

No wonder West Africa was known as the white man's grave! The MMS board for that region repeatedly confirms a life expectancy of about three years after arrival in Africa in the early nineteenth century. Trainee missionaries were not oblivious of this fact. While at Richmond College, they made their own wooden chests in which to transport their belongings on the outbound boat, and began to shape them long and thin, so they could also serve as their coffins. They assumed they wouldn't be coming back alive. Apparently, in the earlier nineteenth century, at their weekly communion service, the principal solemnly read out the names of those whom he learned had died, led a prayer, paused, and then said: "so there are vacancies". At that, he invited any volunteers to remain at the communion rail for prayer. It's said there was never a time when insufficient numbers of volunteers stayed at the rail symbolically declaring, "I'll go." They *went*.

As we will note later, rightful criticism is sometimes levied at mission and missionaries from this era: such is inevitable with almost two centuries of hindsight. But oh that we in our local churches today would embody more of their commitment, their willingness to sacrifice, to *go* and serve, to live and die in order that Christ might be made known among those who do not yet know him. A key thing that those of us who urge churches, old and new, to become more mission-shaped believe is that the mission field today is not only far away but is all around us. Places once profoundly shaped by Christianity are now the places where mission-shaped churches today, like missionary individuals of yesteryear, experience the call of God to *go*. That *going* remains sacrificial and costly.

Pause...

To what extent does your church go?

In what sense does your church go? And to whom?

How could you take a proposal to a leadership meeting within your church to go in some new way? Can you think of creative ways to go and connect with your specific communities?

> ### Go and make disciples.

We note two things about this part of the text. First, that it's one of the most misunderstood (or possibly ignored) commands of Jesus. Second, that "making" Christian disciples today is a vital ministry which is properly given to the church of Christ to undertake. We explore these two statements now.

The command to make disciples is misunderstood because down the decades many churches have read this text to mean "go and make *converts*," so we must reflect briefly on the connection between converts and disciples. Both terms denote a person who is or has become a Christian, but nowadays they aren't understood to be quite the same thing. The term *convert* is closely connected to conversion and is commonly used in relation to explicitly evangelistic activities and their hoped-for outcomes. The term *disciple* is increasingly used to describe a Christian believer whose life is increasingly shaped by their faith in Christ. It isn't that either term is wrong or that there isn't significant overlap between the terms, but mission-shaped churches instinctively focus more on making disciples than converts.

Most local churches will at one time or another have had missions or revivals. They usually involve inviting a visiting speaker or evangelist from out-of-town and asking the congregation to invite their friends and neighbors to attend special meetings. These meetings normally include an invitation to believe in, receive, or give your life to Christ, and it's assumed and expected that those who respond (always a great cause for rejoicing) will demonstrate their new commitment by joining the life of the local church. It's pretty much what happened to both of us and no doubt many readers.

Martyn recalls it like this: I was seventeen. After I went forward, I was taken to a room and counseled by a kindly older man and woman whom I'd never met before. They gave me a booklet (*Journey into Life* by Norman Warren) and explained its illustrations of how Jesus died for my sins on the cross, restored me to God, and now wanted me to give my life to him. They asked if I believed this and if I wanted Jesus in my life as my Savior and Lord, and I said I did. They then led me in a simple prayer, after which the man looked me in the eye and said, "Young man, tonight you've become a Christian. We hope to see you in church on Sunday."

Some of the assumptions going on in this reasonably common account of evangelism and conversion are worth pointing out. First, that this experience and what it entailed—being present at a Christian meeting; indicating a desire to accept Christ; being briefly counselled and prayed with—was itself sufficient to declare a person to be a Christian. Second, a key factor in declaring a person to be a Christian was that they verbally assented to believing various statements of faith. Third, that the expected practical consequence of declaring faith in Jesus was joining and attending church, either for the first time or restarting after a period of back-slidden non-attendance.

Pause...

What is your to faith story?

Did you respond positively or negatively to being evangelized?

It's important to realize that these three assumptions are all rooted in a belief that a society and culture is fundamentally Christian, meaning that large swathes of the population are regarded as Christian or latently Christian, or are lapsed believers having at least a basic working knowledge of the faith they've rejected. In such a society, it's perfectly understandable that evangelists like the late, great Billy Graham could gather tens of thousands of people and invite them to get out of their seats, often explicitly assuming a Christian past in his hearers through their homes, families, Sunday schools, youth groups, or colleges. It was a Christian faith which had been sinned away and rejected, so that now they needed to *return* to Jesus. But here's the rub. That's an increasingly inaccurate understanding of contemporary society, and not only in the West, which is now often said to be post-Christian. Today, fewer and fewer folk can be invited to *return* to any Christian past or faith at all. As churchgoing and Christian influences decline, less Christian legacy and knowledge can be assumed in each successive generation.

Similarly, the idea that verbal assent to certain Christian beliefs identifies a person to be a Christian belongs increasingly to a former time, one in which a good deal of Christian knowledge is assumed and upon which personal assent is based. Some refer to this as *tick box religion*. "Do you believe this?" "Yes I do." "And this?" "Yes." "Great! You've passed." (Or, you haven't!) It isn't that right belief is unimportant. Far from it. It's more that verbal assent to faith statements is increasingly rejected today as a sufficient basis for owning, identifying, or assuming Christian faith. It's too cerebral, too un-holistic, too reduced. Today therefore, making Christians requires starting further back, with much less being assumed, whether in the post-Christian west, or in plural-faith contexts in parts of Africa, Asia, and around the world.

Making Christian disciples aspires to more than has often been expected of converts in terms of whole life, lifelong discipleship. Consequently, making disciples rather than simply converts is one of the greatest needs of the church today. No surprise, therefore, that discipleship rather than conversion is the preferred language of mission-shaped churches, the intended outcome of their evangelism, and a key reason for the creation of fresh expressions of church and pioneering ministries.

Pause . . .

To what extent do you recognize the three assumptions made above?

Do you think your church is still shaped as if it lives in a Christian culture?

The assumption that becoming a Christian involves joining a church brings us to the second main statement about this part of the text of the

Great Commission: namely that making Christian disciples today is a vital ministry, *which is properly given to the church of Christ to undertake.* This takes us to a crucial question for churches of all kinds. When people join a local church, does belonging to it enable them to both become Christians *and* grow into mature disciples of Jesus? In truth, many churches today appear to struggle with both. Tragically, belonging to many churches, even over many years, seems to produce too few spiritual calories to successfully undertake this vital responsibility. Indeed, the apparent inability of many inherited churches in historic denominations to make contemporary Christian disciples is a key reason why we need fresh expressions, reimagined evangelism, and mission-shaped church.

Consequently, mission-shaped churches and fresh expressions focus on disciple making. It is the acid test of "church." This almost always involves evangelism in the sense of finding apt and appropriate ways of inviting people to consider following Jesus Christ, which may be contextually traditional or creatively novel. They also design life together in church consciously and purposely around deepening faith and Christian discipleship. That is their deliberate aim and intention. They assume less and seek to offer more.

> **Make disciples
> of all nations.**

In this, their desire and aim is very like that of early Methodists. Methodism was, at its roots, a discipleship and disciple-making movement. Methodist Christians sought to become better disciples of Jesus Christ and sought to offer him to others. This "commission" lay at the heart of what it meant to be a Methodist Christian. No surprise then that the initial structures of Methodism (class meetings, bands, and the like) encouraged and enabled people to do this. The desire for deepening discipleship came first. Structures arose because they served the desired purpose well.

Today, fresh expressions and mission-shaped churches tend to adopt and adapt those insights, activities, approaches, and practices which seem to work best in terms of disciple-making and faith deepening. They tend to be pragmatic, creative, and adaptive. This is a subtle but hugely significant difference in intention with that of many inherited churches, who at least give the impression that the shape of church is set by those who already belong to it and that attendance and giving are evidence of existing discipleship, which is sustained simply by continued attendance and giving. Mission-shaped churches believe that following Jesus is not merely evidenced by habitual churchgoing but is a lifelong journey involving the whole of life and every aspect of life, that Christianity is not merely life enhancing but life transforming, that church is not (as so often portrayed) a group of salespeople for the gospel in a shop called church but rather free samples of God's grace sent into the world.

Pause...

Is the difference between a convert and a disciple accurate in your experience as a churchgoer?

To what extent is the life of your church shaped around making Christian disciples and deepening discipleship?

Sometimes, when translating the words of New Testament Greek into English, the text does us few favors. This is one of them. Nations, in terms of modern nation states, arose (particularly in Europe) at about the same time that people were deciding that this passage in Matthew should be referred to as the Great Commission. In consequence, when we read "nations" that's what most of us think of. It's also one reason why we still think mission is only about going to other places in the world rather than engaging in God's mission in our own neighborhoods. But the New Testament Greek *panta ta ethne* doesn't mean nations in the sense of France or Mexico—or even States like Florida or Maine— but rather means all *peoples*, of all *races* (ethnicities), in all *places*, of all *ages*, and at all *stages* and *conditions* of human life. In short, everyone. Every generation of Christians has trouble with this passage at this point because it offers no help whatsoever with our tendency to identify the people we want to exclude!

Pause...

To whom do we go and serve?

Whether unintentionally or deliberately, who are those to whom we don't go? And why?

More detail is given to Jesus' commission. The key terms in this sentence are *baptizing* and *teaching*. We will explore these here.

Baptizing them in the name of the Father and of the Son and of the Holy Spirit and teaching them to obey everything that I have commanded you.

In the Acts of the Apostles, baptism is administered usually immediately or very quickly to those who profess belief in Christ. Any significant teaching came afterwards, as is suggested here in Matthew's text. Baptism is nearly always associated with the infilling of the Holy Spirit and administered with water in the name of Jesus Christ rather than in the name of the Holy Trinity. That's one reason why some scholars suggest that this reference to the Trinity in Matthew 28 may be a later insertion into the text. But whether this is the case or not, baptism is clearly commanded by the risen Jesus as the rite of initiation into the company of his disciples and is later identified by His church as a dominical sacrament, that is, explicitly commanded by Christ.

From the end of the Apostolic age, near the end of the first century CE, and increasingly over the following two hundred years or so, saw a general trend to reverse the order of baptism and teaching. In all parts of the expanding Christian world, church leaders developed *catechesis*— meaning instruction. This instruction *preceded* baptism. In some places, catechesis lasted a few months, and in others two or three years. Baptism was the goal and end of catechesis. Often taking place at Easter, it served as a key point of declared faith and the official reception of the person into the church of Jesus Christ. Catechesis was usually undertaken in groups and led by a *catechis*—the teacher or instructor. Great figures of early Christian centuries—Justin Martyr, Ambrose, Augustine of Hippo, Cyril of Jerusalem, and Tertullian, for example—all produced hefty material for those being taught, known as *catechumens*. In contexts of hostility and even persecution, catechesis took place in relative secret, just as some Christians in parts of the world still meet today, and was then, as it is now, a potentially costly undertaking. The process of becoming a Christian, marked liturgically by baptism, became a lengthy and serious business.

By the time Christianity first became an approved licensed religion in the early fourth century and most certainly by the time it became the sole authorized religion of the Roman Empire in the late fourth century, the relationship between teaching and baptism had begun to change again. Living in an officially Christian society caused some to delay baptism as late as possible, ideally near death, because they believed baptism washed away sin, and they wanted to be as pure as possible when meeting their maker. But for the large majority of people, baptism took place earlier rather than later in life, no doubt encouraged by the high rate of infant mortality. Baptizing young children and infants of believers started long before the fourth century, often as a natural and understandable consequence of babies being born into families of Christian believers. It began, from this time on, to become the norm. Our concern here is not to outline the respective merits of believers (adult) baptism and infant baptism, but rather to note that the arrival of infant baptism as common practice reversed the normal order of *teaching* and *baptism*. Over a long period and right down to today in very many Christian denominations, instruction in the faith came *after* infant baptism, connected variously in confirmation (the personal affirming of the faith that had been declared over an infant at its baptism), membership classes, or preparation for first communion.

Again, the assumed cultural context is key. In times when Christianity wasn't a dominant or popular religious force but was one faith set in a sea of pagan religions and cults, it was recognized that teaching through catechesis was required in order to become a Christian. But in contexts where Christianity was the assumed norm, the dominant or only authorized faith, simply being born into such a society was sufficient to quickly offer baptism, with teaching assumed to occur naturally as part of being raised in an environment steeped in and shaped by the Christian faith.

Here's the point. Advocates of mission-shaped church believe that in significant ways, our situation today increasingly resembles more the fragile but potentially fruitful context that produced ancient catechesis rather than the cultural dominance and assumptions of Christendom—a culture and society profoundly shaped by Christian faith. Mostly, mission-shaped churches don't get hung up about baptism itself but are deeply convicted of the need for contemporary teaching (catechesis). In terms of baptism, they tend to be pragmatic. They recognize that most neighborhoods are plural, complex places, and include baptized people (as both infants and adults), some of whom are Christians, some who are nominally Christian, and some who have rejected the faith of their baptism altogether. Mission-shaped churches are aware that many local people won't be baptized at all, will know little about Christianity (or any other faith), and may declare no real interest in religion. They know too that some people will be devout followers of a variety of ancient faiths and contemporary spiritualities. They're convinced, therefore, that making Christian disciples in today's plural, varied populations requires something akin to contemporary catechesis. This is a key aspect of assuming less and starting further back.

Of course, in recent decades, some very good resources that assume less and start further back have been produced. We are, however, probably still nearer the beginning than the end of creating effective catechetical tools for today. While it's ludicrous to suggest that we simply translate ancient catechesis and use it, we can find valuable wisdom and insights from this material. For example, teachers knew then, as we are coming to realize, that to enable a human being to move from one understanding of life, the universe, and everything to another is a long, slow, complex journey; hence catechesis sometimes took years. Of course, people can and do invite Jesus into their lives at a moment in time, however, then a lifelong renewal of life begins. Catechesis has been described as moving from darkness to light, because as Christ makes his home in a human life, and the Holy Spirit convicts, illuminates, strengthens, and transforms, the darkness of human life is enlightened, like a spiritual dimmer switch being turned slowly up.

It's also important to realize that ancient catechesis, though it had substance, wasn't like earning a college degree! Yes, there was input and things to learn, but learning came about in varied ways. There was group work, involving sharing, accountability, ministry, and prayer. Homework was assigned, and issues like anger, honoring God, resistance to violence, the nature of obedience, acts of charity, and honesty in business or (if you were a servant) service, appropriate language, and destructive habits were included. Catechumens were not only told what was expected of believers in Christ but also had to begin to live it out, giving an account of how they were getting on at the next meeting. Accountability and trust were crucial. Catechesis was holistic; it was lived learning rather than simply cerebral, mental assent.

The teaching of Jesus followed this same pattern. Traditional classrooms with desks in rows and a teacher writing on a board while silent pupils copy down what's written there wouldn't be what came into the minds of Jesus' disciples when Jesus said, *teaching them*. . . . Instead, they knew they were being asked to teach others the way they had themselves been taught by Jesus: following their Rabbi (master), heeding his words, witnessing his deeds, receiving his challenging teaching, and being with him through a whole variety of life-changing experiences. In this same way, mission-shaped churches seek to be communities of discipleship and learning, places where together people learn not only *about* Jesus but learn how to become *like* Jesus.

Pause...

What would it mean for your congregation to assume less and start further back?

What do you think contemporary catechesis should consist of? How might it best enable people to not just learn about Jesus, but to learn how to become more like Jesus?

What do you think are the main differences between a lived faith and a mental assent faith?

One final observation, and it concerns another aspect of the original New Testament Greek text which is hard to capture in English. English tends to make the Great Commission sound linear, progressing from one stage to another. You go—to somewhere. And there, you start to make disciples, by baptizing and teaching them. The *koine* Greek text suggests a more fluid, integrated thing. As you are going, and wherever you go, be about discipling, baptizing, and teaching. Mission-shaped churches understand themselves and their ministry in this way. By being themselves, this is what they are about. Going and making disciples isn't what you choose to do from time to time, when you feel like it, or during a week of revival. This is what you were created for, an indispensable part of worshipping God in spirit and in truth.

Pause...

How well does this fluid way of understanding the Great Commission describe your local church?

How might your church go about adopting a fluid way of obeying the Great Commission?

> And remember, I am with you
> always, to the end of the age.

This promise has sustained disciples and missionaries down through the ages. Christ, risen from the dead, is with his disciples. We're probably meant to remember the name given to Jesus before his birth by the angel, recorded only in Matthew. He is to be called Emmanuel which means God is with us (1:23). So here, right at the end of Matthew's Gospel, Jesus, Emmanuel, says "I am with you."

We want to end these reflections on this passage with a small heresy! Is this a *conditional* promise? We quickly grasp the promise that Jesus is with us always. It's a marvelous promise and one we have both hung onto by our spiritual fingernails more than once. But might the nature of the Greek text have Jesus saying: *if* you (my disciples) go, and *if* as you are going you make disciples of everyone everywhere, and *if* in doing so you are baptizing them and teaching everything I've commanded you, *then,* I will be with you always. In which case, to be a church community obedient to and engaged in the Great Commission is the best and most certain way to inherit the promise of knowing that Christ is with us always.

To conclude this chapter, we return to the large wooden boards in London listing the names of Methodist missionaries around the world. Martyn recounts the first time he saw them.

A good friend was showing them to me and explaining their story and context. "When did they die?" my friend suddenly asked me. Taken aback, I thought it was a trick question, but played the game. "It's in the last column, surely", I replied, pointing at a board. "J. H. Wayte, entered college in 1844 and died in 1846." My friend nodded. "You're right," he said, then added quietly, "but I think they also 'died' when they stayed behind after taking communion at Richmond College, or possibly when they first said, 'yes' to Jesus Christ."

Beyond all the logic and persuasion (which is clearly not so logical or persuasive that all local churches willingly and radically place becoming mission-shaped before all else, because most still don't) becoming mission-shaped churches involves a change of heart about *ownership and identity*. It involves a recognition that we (as disciples of Christ) are not our own, and the church ("our" church as we often understandably refer to it) isn't really "ours" either. Both we and it belong to Christ. This is the fundamental realization of the eleven disciples on the mountain, whether those we never hear of again or those whose witness and ministry are recounted in the Acts and elsewhere in the New Testament. They're not, any more than we are, intellectually bullied or spiritually guilt-tripped into embarking reluctantly on the Great Commission (though they falter a bit at first, it's true, as we'll see in a later study in Acts). Theirs is, first and foremost, a response of grateful commitment to Christ who has their love and their loyalty, and consequently their willing, glad obedience. Likewise, love of Christ, and willing glad obedience is the necessary starting place for church congregations who resolve to become more mission-shaped and fertile with good evangelism and fresh expressions.

The Great Commission in the Gospels

Introducing the Idea

In this chapter, we draw upon the work of the late Uruguayan Methodist scholar Mortimer Arias, whose writings are valued by us both. Though not alone in doing so, Arias suggested that a Great Commission can be found not only in Matthew but in each of the Gospels. We have found this approach helpful and inspiring and believe that taken together, the Gospels offer a richer understanding of both the commission of Christ to his followers and the *missio Dei*. In this chapter, we outline what we are going to call the commission of Christ in all four Gospels, paying particular attention to themes and insights that help congregations seeking to be more mission-shaped, authentically evangelistic, and who are desiring to bring to birth many and varied fresh expressions of church.

Readers might expect this chapter to treat a *specific* passage in Mark, Luke, and John in much the same way as we've just focused on Matthew 28:18-20. But not quite, because an essential difference in understanding and approach needs to be recognized. The suggestion that a Great Commission or commission of Christ can be found in each Gospel isn't primarily about identifying a *specific* text as the Great Commission in Mark (or Luke or John). Rather, it's the suggestion that all four Gospels are, *in their entirety,* missional and evangelistic in nature. Consequently, the commission of Christ arises from each Gospel as a whole. Certainly, there are particular texts that best articulate the commission of Christ found in each Gospel. But that's different from identifying a specific proof text as the Great Commission, which may possibly be a text that *misrepresents* the commission of Christ identified *throughout* that Gospel. So, the particular passages to which we draw attention are best seen as *illustrative* of the commission of Christ found throughout that Gospel rather than *definitive,* stand-alone Great Commissions.

The idea that a mission and commission given by Jesus to his followers can be discerned in each Gospel relies on methods of approaching and understanding the Gospels used by biblical scholars for decades. It's assumed and accepted that the evangelists—a common but not unimportant term for the writers of the four Gospels—presented their material in particular ways for particular reasons and purposes. Put simply, each Gospel is the work of those who believed in Jesus and sought to live according to his teachings and instructions in specific religious, social, and cultural contexts. So, when you read it, you can discern something of what they believed about Jesus and how they interpreted his teaching and his instructions in situ. You read not only a kind of biographical story of Jesus but also the mission statement of those who believe and follow him. As the end of John's Gospel puts it, "these things are written that you might believe that Jesus is the Messiah, the Son of God, and that through believing you may have life in his name." (John 20:31). That's a key reason why that Gospel is as it is.

In all four Gospels, it's clear that Jesus' own life, ministry, and mission is the primary source of the life, ministry, and mission of his infant church. How the stories about Jesus are collected and presented, interpreted, and applied give each Gospel its unique flavor and tone. It's possible to discern not only how the Gospel writers (and the Christian communities they belonged to) understood the mission and ministry of Jesus, but also how they understood the ministry and mission *given to them* by Jesus. In this way, the Gospels can deepen our own understanding of the *missio Dei*, the commission of Christ, and the mission given to us who believe in him and seek to follow him today. This is vitally important for both those convinced and those not yet convinced about the critical need for mission-shaped churches, authentic evangelism, and an abundant explosion of fresh expressions.

Pause...

Share together and help one another clarify the distinction between one stand-alone text being the Great Commission and certain texts illustrating the commission of Christ discerned throughout the whole Gospel.

The Commission of Christ in Matthew

Though it might seem odd, we start with Matthew. Odd because we've already reflected on the Great Commission in that Gospel in the previous chapter. However, here, in light of the different approach just outlined, we seek to discern the commission of Christ found in the whole Gospel. Is Matthew 28:16-20 a helpful and accurate distillation of the commission of Christ found throughout that Gospel, or not?

Discipleship and Teaching

Matthew's Gospel focuses deeply on the *discipleship* of Christ. Jesus' teaching is regularly directed at his disciples and is designed to form and shape disciples. It's commonly thought that Matthew is a converted Jewish scribe or rabbi who believes Jesus to be the supreme teacher of the new Law, just as Moses was the teacher of the old. "You have heard it said, 'you shall not . . . ,' but I say to you," says Jesus repeatedly in the Sermon on the Mount. The fact that the Gospel seems to present five blocks of Jesus' teaching, deliberately resonant with the five books of Law in the Old Testament—the Torah—strengthens this suggestion. So does the common view that the Gospel was originally designed as a teaching manual—catechesis—for new Christians. We should not be surprised that the focus of the Great Commission in Matthew 28:19-20 is about making disciples and that an essential ingredient in disciple making is teaching.

Teaching What?

"Teaching them to obey everything that I have commanded you" said Jesus to his disciples on the mountain. (Matthew 28:20) Fine; but what does that mean? What does it include? We get little help from the Great Commission text itself, and this has permitted some to promote their own pet ideas about what Jesus taught and commanded. We need the whole of Matthew's Gospel to enlighten us.

Matthew prefers the phrase "the kingdom of heaven" to "the kingdom of God" and regards this to be the essential theme of Jesus' teaching. We mustn't think that by replacing God with heaven Matthew is disputing it is in fact *God's* kingdom. Rather, because Jesus Christ is Messiah, the new Moses, Emmanuel, then teaching what Jesus taught *and* teaching about him *is* teaching about the kingdom of heaven. The kingdom of heaven is the thematic thread running through the Sermon on the Mount and especially the beatitudes. It's the subject of many of Jesus' parables collected in Matthew. The kingdom of heaven is clearly one of both personal and social righteousness. It is, as Jesus makes clear to Pharisees and hearers alike, about both inside and outside righteousness. Repeatedly, Matthew records Jesus talking about the poor, the weary and overburdened, the powerless, the lowest, and the least of all. So, when Jesus commands his disciples to make disciples of all peoples, they would be under no illusion that people such as these needed to be included.

Discipleship and Obedience

Disciples are made not only through being taught, but also by *obeying* their teacher: "teaching them to *obey* everything that I have commanded you" (Matthew 28:20, emphasis ours). In Matthew, disciples are those who both believe and obediently live out the Gospel of Christ. They are imitators of their Rabbi master and teacher because only when practiced is teaching truly learned. If Jesus says, "go, and do this, and do it like this . . . ," then disciples do it. They obey even when it involves suffering, and Matthew is clear that discipleship involves suffering, just as Jesus suffered. There's always opposition, as Jesus regularly encountered, but that doesn't absolve disciples from being obedient. There's no promise of earthly prosperity, success, or physical protection; there is only a call to faithfulness. Their obedience to Jesus is akin to Jesus' own obedience to the Father. Though there is the precious promise that in obeying and going and making disciples, Jesus will always be present with his disciples.

Discipleship as Loving Obedience

As we noted earlier, the text of Matthew's Great Commission, with its clear commands, has led some to suggest that the Christian mission is essentially undertaken in a state of fear. "We don't really want to do it, but we dare not do it." Again, Matthew's Gospel—as a whole—helps us. It provides a longer, broader, deeper account of the relationship between Jesus and his disciples. Matthew absolutely suggests there is doubt and fear—in the sense of being awestruck—as the risen Jesus appears to the disciples on the mountain. How could it not be so? But by reading the Gospel in its entirety—rather than simply isolating the last few verses of it—the love of Jesus for his disciples is abundantly clear. Despite regular setbacks, they hold a deep love for him and a willing, honest desire to obey him as a response to that committed love. This is crucially important. The disciples don't begin to undertake the Great Commission unwillingly or out of fear, nor should we who follow them. Their motivation and desire is that other people can and should experience the risen, living Lord. They believe—truly believe. Often, we act as though we're not very certain at all that following and serving him is a right and wonderful thing, that it changes lives and life for the better, and consequently transforms the world for good. We must strive to retrieve and retain such motivation for authentic mission-shaped evangelism.

Discipleship for Whom?

In a religious and cultural context in which Jews (as God's chosen people) were usually assumed to be born rather than made, Matthew contends that Christian disciples are made rather than born. Whether a person had to effectively become a Jew before they could become a disciple of Christ was a contentious issue in the earliest church and Matthew's Gospel reflects that—as does Acts and several New Testament epistles. Matthew is sometimes called the Jewish Gospel, and some suggest that Jesus' focus on the house of Israel in earlier chapters of this Gospel mean that his mission is primarily (possibly only) to the Jews. However, Jesus' command to go to all peoples (*panta ta ethne*) clearly affirms a mission to everyone. It's Matthew alone who tells of Magi from the East coming to pay homage to the infant Christ, and only he and Mark have the risen Jesus telling the disciples to go to *Galilee*, a much more Gentile-populated area than Jerusalem. In short, Matthew's gospel declares that the way is open for *anyone* to become Christ's disciple. It's not a thing determined by birth or limited to one faith grouping.

So, was the previous chapter on Matthew's Great Commission in 28:16-20 pointless? No. Rather, it is a key text that *illustrates accurately* the commission of Christ found throughout Matthew's Gospel. It is, however, a text enriched by being understood in that wider context, and at points helpfully clarified and expanded.

> Pause . . .
>
> "You have heard it said . . . But I say to you . . ." What new (old) things do you think you need to hear Jesus saying to you today?

"Teaching them to obey everything that I have commanded you..." What are the teachings of Jesus that you tend to focus upon in your congregation?

What is the evidence that this teaching—in word and deed—is effective in terms of making new disciples and/or deepening the discipleship of long-time members of the congregation?

What does inside and outside holiness look like in your congregation?

"Do you love me?" To what extent do you think your church is engaging in witness and mission, disciple making, and evangelism from a sense of duty, fear, and love?

Do you think your church puts limits on people who can be invited to become disciples of Jesus?

The Commission of Christ in Mark

What about Mark's gospel? As in Matthew, a passage explicitly containing a commission of Christ comes at the end of the Gospel (Mark 16:15-20).

> [Jesus] said to them, "Go into all the world and proclaim the good news to the whole creation. The one who believes and is baptized will be saved; but the one who does not believe will be condemned. And these signs will accompany those who believe: by using my name they will cast out demons; they will speak in new tongues; they will pick up snakes in their hands, and if they drink any deadly thing, it will not hurt them; they will lay their hands on the sick, and they will recover." . . . And they went out and proclaimed the good news everywhere, while the Lord worked with them and confirmed the message by the signs that accompanied it.

We can see an immediate issue with this passage, coming as it does in the so-called long ending of Mark's Gospel. All modern Bible translations suggest that this text is a slightly later addition, most likely by a different writer than the Mark of the Gospel up to this point. So, if it isn't that Mark, does it count? And if it doesn't count, is there any commission of Christ in Mark's Gospel at all? We suggest that there is and that it does count. If Mark's Gospel itself is understood to be an evangelistic mission document, and if this passage illustrates well the commission of Jesus discerned within it, then whether it's by a later editor or not is irrelevant. We proceed on this basis.

The actual commission of Jesus in this passage, when stripped of the narrative surrounding it, is brief. "Go into all the world and proclaim the good news to the whole creation." We note immediately that there's no escape from the command to Jesus' disciples to go. It's not a quirky notion found only in Matthew. We also note that the command to go to the whole creation is more helpful than all nations or even all peoples.

The late, great professor and practitioner of preaching, Fred Craddock, told his students to address right away anything about a text that might jar in the minds of its hearers. Otherwise, it will irritate them, so that they can't easily receive the rest of the sermon. In relation to this particular text then, we must note that some readers will be more familiar with "Go into all the world and preach the gospel . . ." rather than "proclaim the good news", both of which are found in various Bible translations. Indeed, so well-known is the phrase "preach the gospel" that some insert it into Matthew's Great Commission even though it's not found there. We've chosen to use "proclaim the good news" here because despite the old saying often attributed to St. Francis of Assisi: "Preach the gospel always, and when necessary use words,", what preaching is normally understood to be isn't all of what proclamation means. While proclamation certainly includes preaching, there is an important distinction to make at this point; and we hope, as Craddock suggested, it enables readers to receive the rest of this section without much irritation!

Proclamation

"Proclaim the good news," commands Jesus. "And they went out and proclaimed the good news everywhere." The proclamation of good news is a prominent theme in Mark. The Gospel begins, "The beginning of the good news of Jesus Christ, the Son of God" (Mark 1:1), indicating that the writer(s) intend the whole Gospel to be understood as gospel proclamation. In Mark, Jesus understands his own mission as the proclamation of the kingdom of God (his preferred term rather than Matthew's kingdom of heaven).

In Deed and Word

This passage in Mark 16 makes clear that the proclamation expected of those receiving Christ's commission involves both deeds and words, which is no surprise as Jesus' mission and ministry is a wonderful model of such. In Mark's Gospel particularly, Jesus' deeds often take precedence over his words, usually with teaching coming after Jesus performs a miracle, healing, or exorcism. Jesus appears to regard his deeds as *themselves* proclamatory of the kingdom of God, rather than simply attention-seeking devices enabling him to *teach* verbally about God's kingdom. When he heals someone, it's about meeting their needs rather than demonstrating his power, about affirming their own often frail faith rather than generating faith by performing miracles. When Jesus performs exorcisms, it's because he's against anything and everything that harms, binds, or oppresses human life. When he feeds crowds, he's declaring that the kingdom of God isn't pie in the sky when you die, but concerns human health, thriving, and wholeness, here and now.

Of course, all churches believe that proclaiming God's kingdom happens by words and deeds. But whether by instinct or careful reflection, most fresh expressions of church tend to *act* Christianly and humanly first (through a variety of both straightforward and innovative practical ministries of service) and *speak* of faith in an interwoven way, usually within the natural environment created by such ministries. This is the reverse of some more traditional ways of proclamatory evangelism.

Consequently, most people who encounter fresh expressions of church do so first through its kingdom deeds before hearing its gospel words. At their best, mission-shaped churches not only love and serve people in authentic ways, but in ways that enable those very folk to know and believe that they have integrity, respect, value, and worth. People are not made to feel like mere objects of charity so that Christians can do their off-putting "I'm-helping-you-so-that-you-know-I-really-love-God" thing.

Mission-shaped churches and fresh expressions also place great emphasis on apt and timely ways of proclaiming the gospel using *words*. This happens usually in casual environments, in neutral places and spaces, by mutual sharing and open conversation, often in one-to-one or in small groups. This is their preferred style, rather than the more formal, church building based, one person preaching to many, often rather one-sided exchanges still perpetuated by many inherited churches.

Pause . . .

Do you think your church tends to focus on preaching or proclamation?

What is the relationship between gospel words and deeds in your church?

Do the words and deeds agree about the nature of the gospel being proclaimed, or do they declare different things? If so, what are those "things"?

When a new person or family comes to join your church family, what do you think the body language of the congregation encourages them to say and be in order for them to join you?

(If new folk are available and willing, ask them about this, and listen very carefully to what they say. Ask them also whether it was easy or difficult to join your congregation—remembering that the people who found you difficult to join are most likely not still there to ask!)

Does your congregation have casual environments and neutral places and spaces, in which open conversation and mutual sharing takes place? If not, are you going to go about creating such places and spaces?

Which Brings about Confrontation and Controversy

Another thing made plain in Mark's gospel is that announcing God's kingdom inevitably denounces everything that works against God's kingdom. The very deeds of the kingdom Jesus demonstrates constantly place him in situations of confrontation and controversy. He heals on the Sabbath. He touches lepers. He talks with women. He mingles and eats with sinners. He forgives sins. He associates with Gentiles. He calls people— even important people—to account. Jesus doesn't go around deliberately looking for trouble, saying, "Now, which Pharisee can I offend today?" God's kingdom by its very nature challenges everything else. When that which is life-giving, just, and holy is proclaimed, that which destroys life, is unjust, and unholy is utterly rejected. By proclaiming the kingdom, Jesus is driven away from his home area, constantly castigated by religious people, and in the end, is arrested, tried, and crucified. Even Jesus was unable to avoid misunderstanding, controversy, and opposition.

This is an uncomfortable reality of proclamation and challenges all Christians and every congregation, especially those living in parts of the world where Christianity is weak, vilified, and persecuted. An important aspect of being mission-shaped today is not to seek to avoid all controversy and opposition, but to take care that when it arises, it is *for right or better* reasons, rather than *wrong* or *poorer* reasons. Sadly, some Christians and churches seem to relish confrontation, and their speech and actions appear designed to court and create it. Who hasn't heard the open-air Christian speaker preaching love like hate? Who hasn't encountered hostility, bigotry, insults, rejection, cruelty, hypocrisy, discrimination, racism, or sexism dressed up in the language of earnest Christianity? Who hasn't met those Christians who think that the greater the level of opposition to what they say and do, the more right it is to say and do it? This is proclamation gone wrong, and people are right to confront and oppose it. What a far cry from the attitudes and actions of Jesus this is! Jesus generates confrontation and opposition because he is God's compassionate, redemptive love in action. How can it be right that the ministry and mission of those who bear Christ's name is often so different in tone and nature to his? How often do Christians regard people simply as sinners, whereas Jesus regarded human beings not only as sinners, but also as the sinned against; not simply as violators of God's laws, but also as the violated and supremely loved by their creator. It's discerning and affirming love rather than discriminating love that characterizes the best mission and evangelism today. Whatever else the kingdom of God is about, it is always offer before demand, redemption with challenge, healing with acceptance, grace with truth, forgiveness with firmness, mercy and justice with consequences. Ultimately, it can never be anything other than good news. Proclaiming God's kingdom in such a mood and tone won't prevent controversy and opposition, but it will occur for better rather than poorer reasons.

However, poor witness and evangelism is easy to criticize. A harder challenge is posed by the recognition that many churches, particularly but not only in the West, with their long and close associations with power and influence, appear to have lost or deliberately rejected their prophetic, proclamatory role within the community of the good news of God's kingdom. Unlike its Lord, the church is too often mute and even craven in the face of that which opposes or subverts the kingdom of God, that which dehumanizes, exploits, and abuses. Put simply, the church proclaims and protests about some things it probably shouldn't and fails to proclaim and protest about some things it most certainly should.

Shaming the consciences of complacent churches comes through several voices, and we mention just two here. One is the (gentle, sometimes too respectful) voice of the poor, powerless, often despised, and sometimes persecuted people throughout the world, which includes but isn't limited to Christian people. Another is the (disappointed, sometimes angry, sometimes resigned) voice of the many people in our own societies and neighborhoods who regard Christianity and church as completely irrelevant, and even sometimes associate it with the elite and corrupt powers that control and constrain their lives. These two voices, from different people, places, and perspectives, both recognize our passivity and timidity as church much better than we usually allow ourselves to do. They observe our complacent collusion with self-serving processes, unjust systems, exploitative practices, and prejudicial arrangements, and lament our unquestioning silences. They yearn and often strive to shape their world with values and actions resonant with the good news we proclaim and are bewildered at our lack of involvement and support. They recognize the tragic gulf between word and deed in the church of Jesus Christ. In this regard, if only the church gave more good reasons for greater opposition and controversy!

All churches have a long way to go in regard to this challenge. Many mission-shaped and fresh expressions of church seem to relate and connect naturally to groups of people not often found in our more traditional churches. They're also often configured around kingdom ministries of some kind; a congregation living among and including the homeless, a church shaped towards befriending and healthily integrating poor migrants, a Christian group publicly supportive of (or even taking a lead in creating) a credit union or micro-grant-giving body. Fresh expressions often benefit from being less constrained by the perceived need for civic respectability and acceptability. Though they hold no monopoly of these things, fresh expressions are often recognized by others as communities of God's kingdom people rather than congregations of religious people. That's one reason why they're so needed today.

A good gauge of how serious a church is about becoming more mission-shaped is how seriously they take such challenging issues as these.

Pause...

To what extent do you associate your church with controversy and opposition? Does it arise, and if it does, do you think for the right reasons?

The church proclaims and protests about some things it shouldn't and fails to proclaim and protest about many things it should. To what extent do you think this is true of your church?

How do you respond to the two voices of conscience? How do you respond to the fact that some think your church is complacent and self-serving? What can you do about it?

Fresh expressions more than many churches seem to relate and connect naturally to groups of people not often found in our churches. What groups of people not often found in church does your congregation relate and connect naturally to?

Do you think people regard your local church as a community of God's kingdom people or a congregation of religious people? Why or why not?

Signs, Reassurance, and Protection

"And these signs will accompany those who believe. . . ." In Mark's gospel, Jesus is emphatic that signs will accompany believers in him as they go to the whole world proclaiming good news. As part of the longer and later ending of Mark's gospel, many scholars either quickly dismiss this as not the words of Jesus or they try to explain the significance of signs, particularly in relation to handling snakes and drinking poison without being harmed. Our own suggestion is that these various accompanying signs reinforce the two things we've noted about Jesus' mission in Mark so far: that God's kingdom is proclaimed in deeds and words, and that this inevitably brings about controversy and opposition. So, those sent by Jesus will do what he did in his name, because his kingdom mission is theirs also. They will confront and conquer evil and heal the sick. They will also encounter opposition, hostility, and danger (snakes and poison), but they will not be harmed. This is a clear encouragement to be courageous and not let inevitable confrontation prevent or dissuade believers in Jesus to engage in the proclamation of God's kingdom. Like Matthew's promise of Christ's presence, this is Mark's reassurance of Christ's protection.

The strong likelihood however is that Christians in Mark's circles *were* coming to harm. Consequently, we must lay alongside these assurances of safety and protection another theme that lies at the heart of proclaiming the good news to all creation, namely, that it involves proclaiming *both* the *life* of Jesus (whose words and deeds make clear what the kingdom of God is like) *and* his suffering, sacrificial and atoning *death* (through which everyone can enter the kingdom of God).

There is in Mark's gospel a hinge. It doesn't break the gospel in two but bends it and all its contents up to that hinge-point into a different trajectory. The flood of signs of the kingdom in terms of Jesus' exorcisms, healings, and miracles—and to some extent his parables about the kingdom of God—largely dry up. Instead, Jesus begins to talk about his sufferings and death and later hints at his rising from the dead. Several chapters in Mark focus on his going to Jerusalem and what happens there. There can be no doubt therefore that when the risen Jesus tells his disciples to proclaim the good news of the kingdom, they understand that this includes proclaiming and living out his life-giving, kingdom-accessing *death*. Similarly, later generations of believers reading or hearing this gospel and its commission would recognize that proclaiming the good news involves imitating Christ through kingdom words and deeds, encountering opposition and danger, *and*—a third aspect—being suffering servants of the Suffering Servant to the point of laying down their lives if necessary. In this broader context of the nature of discipleship and mission, and the reality of hostility and persecution directed at Christians, the promise of immunity from snakes and poison was probably recognized as a promise that no *ultimate* harm would befall believers. Even in death, their eternal salvation and safety would be assured.

Many people regard Christianity as a death religion, concerned primarily and mostly with what happens after you die. Mission-shaped churches and fresh expressions are clear about the saving nature of Christ's death and the promise of eternal life, but more than many inherited churches, they tend to put greater emphasis upon Christianity as *life-affirming*, a life to be lived now. In subtle ways, this often has the effect of changing the mood and tone of belonging to that congregation, which is experienced as exciting, challenging, and fulfilling. This stands in sharp contrast to the harsh reality that many churches are too shaped by an unquestioned dull routine, a laudable but heavy sense of duty, and a lack of authentic engagement with the real needs and lives of many human beings.

We conclude this brief exploration of the commission of Christ in Mark by revisiting the proclamation of good news in relation to evangelism. Many churches have, if they're honest with themselves, effectively given up on evangelism. They're far happier with talk of mission as kingdom ministries to others, offering support and donations, than with the irritating, persistent notion that Jesus Christ is to be incarnationally proclaimed as Lord and Savior of all. Mission-shaped churches and fresh expressions don't give up on evangelism. That doesn't mean that they persist with those traditional models of evangelism which they recognize are less effective and more counterproductive than they once were. They reimagine evangelism rather than abandon it. They find ways of offering Christ that have appeal and relevance, attraction and substance. Their invitations to people to accept Jesus Christ usually arise out of warm relationships already built rather than cold call and pompous pulpit encounters. Like all churches, fresh expressions connect becoming a Christian with becoming part of the Christian community. But in their case, it is a community which has already demonstrated love, acceptance, and welcome to those to whom they offer Christ. A fresh expressions community is one that's so passionate, vibrant, and committed about being Christian that those entering its orbit know and accept it from the outset as a place where faith is created, developed, deepened, and shared, where lives and living are changed for the better. Church communities must sufficiently believe and model the faith they profess. If they don't, for all the value to existing members and the deep love in which it is held by many, a local church won't be able to become a home or a base camp in which many contemporary people choosing to follow Jesus can thrive. A simple but key difference between an inherited church and one seeking seriously to be mission-shaped is the extent to which they recognize and respond positively and selflessly to such realities.

Pause . . .

What are the main signs that you are a company of believers in Jesus Christ? What do you think people see first about you?

To what extent is suffering servants of The Suffering Servant a description of your life as a congregation? In what ways?

Exciting, challenging, and fulfilling or a dull routine and a heavy sense of duty? What is God saying to you about your life together?

Have you given up on evangelism? What would it mean to reimagine evangelism in your local church?

The Commission of Christ in Luke

Then he said to them, 'These are my words that I spoke to you while I was still with you—that everything written about me in the law of Moses, the prophets, and the psalms must be fulfilled.' Then he opened their minds to understand the scriptures, and he said to them, 'Thus it is written, that the Messiah is to suffer and to rise from the dead on the third day, and that repentance and forgiveness of sins is to be proclaimed in his name to all nations, beginning from Jerusalem. You are witnesses of these things. And see, I am sending upon you what my Father promised; so stay here in the city until you have been clothed with power from on high.' (Luke 24:44-49, NRSV)

In terms of a commission by the risen Jesus to his disciples, this is a key passage. They are to be his witnesses but need first to have their minds opened by him to understand the scriptures about him. He is the

Messiah, and his suffering and resurrection (his death is implied here, rather than specified) were foretold and have now come about. His sufferings and crucifixion were meant to happen and aren't a catastrophic mistake somehow rectified by the resurrection. Having witnessed these things and believing who he is, *repentance and forgiveness of sins* must now be proclaimed in his name, starting in Jerusalem, then to all nations. But for the time being, the disciples must stay in Jerusalem and wait for *power from on high*, a clear reference to the Holy Spirit, without which they can't be or do what Jesus asks of them.

Does this passage accurately resonate with the commission of Christ found in Luke's gospel as a whole—and even the book of Acts as Luke's sequel to the gospel? If so, these themes should be plain and evident throughout the gospel. First, the gospel will emphasize being witnesses to Jesus the Messiah, whose life, death, and resurrection is understood in light of the whole of scripture. Second, it will focus on proclaiming repentance and the forgiveness of sins. And third, the Gospel will recognize that this all requires the promised help and presence of the Holy Spirit. We will look briefly at each of these suppositions.

Witnesses of These Things

The opening paragraph (Luke 1:1-4) sets out the overall aim and intention of the Gospel. After thoroughly investigating accounts about Jesus handed down by *"eyewitnesses and servants of the Word,"* Luke offers his own *"orderly account."* It is dedicated to Theophilus, as is the book of Acts. Theophilus means lover of God in New Testament Greek. He was possibly an eminent convert. Luke's intention is that this lover of God, and indeed everyone else who reads his Gospel, "may know the truth concerning the things about which you have been instructed." At the beginning of Acts, Luke summarizes his Gospel: "In my first book, Theophilus, I wrote about all that Jesus did and taught from the beginning until the day he was taken up to heaven." (Acts 1:1-2.) Luke's Gospel is itself a *witness of these things* just as the risen Jesus commanded his disciples to be. The whole Gospel presents the truth of who Jesus is, his teaching, life, suffering, death, and resurrection. No surprise then that Luke alone tells how the risen Jesus joins disillusioned disciples on the road to Emmaus and *opens the scriptures to them* (24:32), or that Luke alone tells us that Jesus *presented himself alive to them by many convincing proofs, appearing to them during forty days and speaking about the kingdom of God* (Acts 1:3). John's Gospel is written that we "might have life in all its fullness." Luke's Gospel is written that we might know the truth about Jesus the Messiah and bear witness to him.

One of the criticisms sometimes levied at fresh expressions is that they are church-lite. That there's too much informality, no serious reading or study of the scriptures, no proper worship, and so on. This may well be the case in some instances, but we've found the reverse to be more common. Very often the congregations of fresh expressions of church have a deep desire to understand the scriptures, a large appetite for worship, teaching, and sharing and, notably, bearing witness to their faith. Indeed, in our experience, fresh expressions tend to engage with complex questions and issues more seriously and thoroughly than do many inherited churches.

For example, when folk with very limited Christian knowledge or experience choose to become Christian believers, what is it that they need to know and experience to enable them to be so? To what extent does life in the fresh expression need to translate Christian beliefs, belonging, and behavior into the existing worldview of the new disciple? And conversely, to what extent does the new disciple need to begin to learn the language and life of the Christian church? What is expected of them that begins to mold them as disciples of Christ? How much of this expected change is essentially about authentic Christian discipleship and how much is about conforming to the culture of what disciples are "supposed to be like" in this church?

It's a balancing act, one which Christians through the centuries have tried to walk steadily and wisely, and one which faces all churches today. In their book *Resident Aliens*, Hauerwas and Willimon comment, "Alas, in leaning over to speak to the modern world, we had fallen in"[1] suggesting that there is often more capitulation than transformation. Mis-

---

[1] Stanley Hauerwas and William Willimon, *Resident Aliens: Life in the Christian Colony* (Nashville: Abdington Press, 1989), 26.

sion-shaped churches and fresh expressions don't always get the balancing act right, but more than many churches, they recognize, understand, and commit themselves to the essential task of being a living environment in which contemporary people can become authentic Christian believers. This often involves recasting teaching, prayer, worship, or witness in ways, spaces, and tones that help enable the miracle of Christian transformation to occur.

Pause...

In what ways does our congregation bear witness to who Jesus is?

How are we doing in relation to this balancing act of not falling in, while enabling new people to become contemporary disciples of Jesus?

How much of what we think and expect of a new Christian is authentic, essential gospel, and how much is merely our own preferred ways and culture?

A Jubilee of Metanoia and Aphesis

The second theme of the commission of Christ in Luke's Gospel is the proclamation of repentance and forgiveness of sins. Such proclamation is found throughout the Gospel and in Acts. Stories of the apostles inviting people to repent and believe the good news of Jesus Christ are common. The New Testament Greek word used in Luke 24 and often translated as repentance is *metanoia*, which means a complete change of heart and way of life arising from a realization of sin and need, leading to a turning to Christ. The rarer New Testament Greek word used by Luke translated as forgiveness is *aphesis*. Rather than a blithe "I'm sorry," responded to by a quick "it's alright," *aphesis* signals powerful release, a gracious costly pardon, the bringing of real freedom and liberty, putting right something profoundly wrong. These themes are common in Jesus' teaching and

actions and are nowhere presented more clearly than in his manifesto in
Luke 4: 18-19:

> The Spirit of the Lord is upon me,
>   because he has anointed me
>   to bring good news to the poor.
> He has sent me to proclaim release to the captives
>   and recovery of sight to the blind,
>   to let the oppressed go free,
> to proclaim the year of the Lord's favor.

This passage from Isaiah, adopted and slightly adapted by Jesus,
is associated with the Old Testament theme of Jubilee—a special year
occurring every fifty years focusing on new starts, forgiveness, and
liberation—*the year of the Lord's favor*. Land was to be restored and
returned to those who had lost it or had it taken unfairly from them.
Slaves were to be set free and debts cancelled. It was understood as God's
chosen way of enabling fresh beginnings, righting wrongs, addressing
accumulated injustices, and restoring relationships. Essentially, Jubilee
concerned *metanoia* and *aphesis*. The full measure of Jubilee in terms of
these intentions and actions rarely, if ever, occurred in biblical history.
But Luke is clear that they are being and will be fulfilled in Jesus Christ,
who not only proclaims Jubilee themes, but *is* God's incarnated Jubilee.

An Inclusive and Holistic Jubilee

Not surprisingly, Jesus' Jubilee manifesto in Luke 4 is understood in various ways today. Some have suggested it's essentially *spiritual* teaching and
refers only to the spiritually poor or captives. But this hardly does justice
to the holistic nature of Jesus' ministry and teaching. Others suggest it
was intended *literally*: that Jesus was publicly proposing a Jubilee year.
His pleas fell on deaf ears. The most common and better understanding
of this Jubilee manifesto is that it makes clear what God desires for all
humankind, that God's kingdom is Jubilee-shaped and therefore marked
by *metanoia* and *aphesis*. Like Matthew and Mark, Luke's Gospel portrays
Jesus' mission as essentially the proclaiming of God's kingdom. But Luke

is particularly explicit that God's kingdom has real political, social, ethical, pastoral, and religious dimensions. Jesus' Jubilee manifesto is a key
biblical text for many Christians. It is often applied to—and owned by—
poor and marginalized peoples as a gospel of socio-political liberation.
Equally, it is often used to urge privileged peoples to change their lives
and seek repentance and forgiveness of sins. We must note, however, that
Jesus doesn't offer the luxury of two gospels, one of repentance directed
at the rich and one of forgiveness directed at the poor. The gospel is the
challenge and offer of both *metanoia* and *aphesis* to everyone in every
circumstance.

The Jubilee proclaimed through Jesus' words and deeds is wonderfully inclusive and holistic. Luke's Gospel especially contains story after
story of Jesus with outcasts and sinners. Lepers, tax-collectors, Samaritans, women, the economically, spiritually, and socially poor, and the rich
all feature prominently. The Good Samaritan (a parable found only in
Luke) is good because of his unanticipated humanity, mercy, and generosity towards someone he isn't supposed to care about (Luke 10: 25-37).
Jesus' encounter with rich Zacchaeus the tax-collector (also found only in
Luke) is a classic tale of *metanoia* and *aphesis*, a life turned around and set
free evidenced by radical changes in lifestyle which, in turn, frees others
(Luke 19:1-10). Similarly, Jesus' healings in Luke are also presented in
terms of Jubilee. They are about the liberation of body, mind, spirit, and
relationships—they are about restoration of life.

Throughout Jesus' ministry and mission, calls for repentance and
offers of forgiveness of sins are indissoluble from compassion, love, and a
genuine interest in and concern about the individual. Luke particularly
notices that contrition, gratitude, and generosity are common responses
to Jesus, particularly by outcasts and sinners. They are marks of *metanoia*
and *aphesis*. Only one of the ten lepers healed by Jesus returns to offer his
thanks and, we are told pointedly, he is a Samaritan (Luke 17:15). A sinful
(and probably abused) woman pours expensive perfume over Jesus' feet,
wipes them with tears of gratitude, kisses them repeatedly, and dries them
with her hair (Luke 7:37-38). Zacchaeus does what the rich young ruler
couldn't do (Luke puts the two stories closely together so we'll notice

their different responses) and demonstrates his transformational salvation in terms of tangible generosity and deep gratitude.

Like inherited churches, mission-shaped churches and fresh expressions come in lots of shapes and sizes. There's no blueprint. One size does not fit all. But in many contextually savvy ways, mission-shaped churches find winsome and authentic means of presenting both repentance and forgiveness of sins to contemporary people. Repentance is a difficult concept for many churches today. It assumes human sinfulness, and we all know of churches who claim: "we don't do sin"! By this, they often mean that they have rejected hellfire and damnation preaching and stopped regarding people as first and foremost sinners who need to repent by publicly bewailing their wickedness. Many mission-shaped churches and fresh expressions similarly abandon this approach. But unlike some churches, they don't effectively abandon references to sin or remove mention of the consequential need for repentance. Rather they recast and re-present the transformative offer and demand inherent in *metanoia* and *aphesis*: terms which, it will have been recognized already, are much richer in meaning than repentance and forgiveness are often understood to be by many Christian congregations.

Mission-shaped churches rarely tend to start with a person's sinfulness, unless the person does so themself. But they do talk about honesty, renewal, and turnaround. They speak of God's desire to make people whole and free, of strength being given to enable any person to turn to Christ, and the real possibility of profound and lasting change and transformation. They proclaim and embody hope to unchurched people fresh to Christian faith, people who are usually much more concerned about becoming new and better rather than becoming nice and churched. Consequently, much more testimony—of grace given, healing received, and continuing struggles enabled by divine strength—takes place in such congregations. There also tends to be more rejoicing and gratitude.

The effect of adopting such an attitude towards others is deceptive and easily underestimated. During the *Decade of Evangelism* (the 1990s) in the United Kingdom, a major research project was undertaken and published in a book titled *Finding Faith Today*. It involved interviews with several hundred people who at that time had recently come to a living Christian faith. Some used the language of conversion, some the language of journey. Some marked their new faith by baptism or confirmation, some by bearing testimony. Taken together, the ways that contemporary people find faith become clearer. Some of the factors were unsurprising. For example, very few of us respond positively to the Christian gospel the first time we hear it. Most of us come to say yes to Jesus, because many times, over time, those we like and love and respect show us love, care, and respect. They gently invite and encourage us to follow Jesus Christ, and pray that we will, until we do. Other factors in the book were more surprising. Take, for example, the responses to the question: What have you learned about God since you came to faith? To which there was one dominant response which went something like this: "Before I came to faith, I thought God was unknowable and unfeeling, distant, and remote. I didn't think God was bothered about me or liked me. Now I know that God loves me, accepts me, is close to me, is real to me, and that's changed my life."[2]

Churches that don't abandon all notions of sin or any need for repentance (which, after all, is extremely hard to justify from the Christian scriptures) but do present the possibility of authentic *metanoia* and *aphesis* and create a context and community in which these gospel gifts of Jubilee are expected and celebrated take a major step towards becoming more completely mission-shaped.

Pause...

How does your church congregation understand repentance and forgiveness?

Does your church proclaim regularly the sinfulness of people? If so, how? If not, why not?

What would it mean for your congregation to become more Jubilee-shaped?

---

[2] John Finney, *Finding Faith Today*. (Australia: Bible Society, 1992).

The Promised Holy Spirit

The third theme of the commission of Christ concerns the need of and reliance upon the Holy Spirit. This theme too is found throughout Luke's Gospel and particularly in the transition passages that connect Luke and Acts. Luke, more than the other Gospels, refers to the Holy Spirit, both generally and specifically. Specifically, the Holy Spirit is presented as enabling the recognizing of who Jesus is, bearing witness to him, and proclaiming repentance and forgiveness of sins. For example, it's Luke who tells us most about John the Baptist, who is *filled with the Holy Spirit from birth* (Luke 1:16). John who bears witness to Jesus, recognizes him as the Messiah foretold in the scriptures and proclaims *a baptism of repentance for the forgiveness of sins* (Luke 3:4). It's only Luke who tells about old Simeon and Anna in the Temple when the infant Jesus is consecrated to God. The Holy Spirit rests on them, and they both recognize and bear witness that in this Christ-child, the salvation God has prepared for all people has come. (Luke 2:25-38). Or again, in the variations found in the Gospels about Jesus' temptations in the wilderness, it's Luke who tells us that Jesus is *full of the Holy Spirit* as he enters the desert and that he remains *filled with the power of the Spirit* as he leaves it and goes into Galilee (Luke 4:1 and 14). Then in Galilee, as we've already noted, Jesus begins his Jubilee manifesto with the words *The Spirit of the Lord is upon me.* Many more instances could be given, but two main points are made. First, the Holy Spirit enables what Jesus mandates in Luke 24: recognition of who he is, bearing witness to him, and proclaiming repentance and forgiveness of sins. Second, if Jesus the Messiah requires the presence and help of the Holy Spirit in his mission, how much more do his disciples need the same Holy Spirit to undertake the mission he has given them?

Fresh expressions and mission-shaped churches aren't all charismatic or pentecostal by any means. The assertion that they are all froth and happy clappy is a myth. Some are gritty gatherings. But they do seem to recognize their profound reliance on the Holy Spirit more than many churches. Perhaps it is because they tend to take more holy risks than most congregations. Perhaps their deep engagement with unchurched folk propels them to talk more about the Holy Spirit, about trusting and relying on her. But for whatever reason, fresh expressions are not merely *fresh* because they are young or novel. They are often places of refreshment and excitement in which the Spirit of God seems to enjoy inhabiting and infusing, and in turn is welcomed and celebrated.

Pause...

To what extent does your congregation talk about the Holy Spirit of God?

Do you think your congregation relies upon the Holy Spirit in an open and acknowledged way?

When was the last time your congregation went out on a limb, took a holy risk, and so placed itself in clear need of the help and leading of the Holy Spirit?

We're now able to assert that the three key elements found in Jesus' commission in Luke 24 are indeed found throughout the Gospel. It accurately expresses the commission of Christ throughout the whole text.

Who's Included in Jesus' Commission?

We address just one more issue. Who was Jesus talking to when he gave his commission? Who's included in Jesus' commission according to Luke?

Matthew's Gospel was clear and explicit. Jesus gave his Great Commission to *the eleven*—the twelve disciples minus Judas. By comparison, Luke's commission is vague as to the subjects of it. It begins, "Then he said to them," and it's a reasonable question to ask who "them" might be.

The whole of Luke chapter 24 helps set the scene. In the earlier verses telling of the Resurrection of Jesus, "they" are clearly a group of women. Luke records how *Mary Magdalene, Joanna, Mary the mother of James and the other women* run from the empty tomb to relay what's happened to *the eleven and to all the rest*. There's then the long story of Jesus with two of them walking to Emmaus. They tell the unknown stranger on the road that they were present in Jerusalem earlier that day, heard the story of the women, and note that *some of those who were with us* went to the tomb. But these two followers didn't and are now walking away disconsolately from Jerusalem. That the risen Jesus should spend the day of his resurrection with two dispirited disciples is wonderfully moving. That those disciples should be released from bewilderment, have their eyes and hearts opened to who Jesus is, and restored to life as his witnesses, is wonderful Lukan Jubilee Gospel! The duo return joyfully to Jerusalem and find *the eleven and their companions gathered together*, and it's reasonable to assume that this group is the "them" to whom the risen Jesus appears, offers his peace, invites to touch him to prove he's no ghost, and eats fish with them to prove the point. In which case, it's most likely that this larger group is the "them" to whom Jesus issues his commission.

Rather than simply noting Luke's vagueness as to who is present when Jesus gives his commission, we want to suggest that this vagueness is very likely deliberate. Jesus calls several layers of disciples as recorded in Luke's Gospel. He calls the twelve of course, who are to follow him and become fishers of people. But Luke alone also tells us of the call of the seventy (Luke 10). They are to go ahead of Jesus in pairs, visiting homes and towns, declaring that God's kingdom has come near, healing the sick, and bringing peace. They have no special apostolic authority but clearly have power and report joyfully to Jesus the successes of their mission and ministry in his name. Even at this point in his ministry, Jesus is clearly inviting and even depending on others to expand his own mission. The twelve disciples are often said to represent symbolically the twelve tribes of Israel. Similarly, the seventy (or seventy-two in some translations) are sometimes said to represent the number of the nations in the world (known at the time of Jesus). Taken together, there is a clear suggestion in Luke that the commission of Jesus extends to and includes *everyone*: all nations, all people, the whole of creation.

But in addition to the twelve and the seventy, we see one more layer of those who Luke suggests are explicitly included in the commission of Jesus. They have recognized who he is and bear witness to him. They have experienced, embodied, and proclaimed Jubilee repentance and forgiveness. They are included as those who receive the Holy Spirit: women. Only in Luke are we told that some women accompany Jesus and the twelve, as they *go through cities and villages, proclaiming and bringing the good news of the kingdom of God* (8:1-3). Luke characteristically offers some names: *Mary, called Magdalene . . . Joanna, (the wife of Herod's steward Chuza) and Susanna, and many others.* We note the clear connection with the group of women Luke tells visit the tomb intending to anoint the dead body of Jesus. Some of these women provide for the whole group out of their own resources, suggesting they were people of wealth. Also, we're told that they've been released from evil spirits and healed from diseases. In other words, they are walking witnesses of Jesus' Jubilee mission! These are the semi-visible but profoundly effective disciples of Jesus. They are surely in the larger group of disciples when Jesus stands among them and gives them his commission. Far from being vague, Luke more than any other Gospel, makes clear that there are no exclusions to those invited to be his disciples and to whom he gives his commission. Outcasts and sinners, the marginalized, the poor and the rich, liberated and made whole through *metanoia* and *aphesis*, the twelve and the seventy, women and men, you and your church community are all included in his Jubilee mission.

Church communities that realize this, and embody its truth, inevitably become more mission-shaped.

Pause . . .

Do you think your congregation makes clear that you are each and all—laity and clergy—included in Jesus' commission? If so, how? If not, why not, and how might that inclusion come about?

The Commission of Christ in John

When it was evening on that day, the first day of the week . . .
Jesus came and stood among them and said, "Peace be with
you." After he said this, he showed them his hands and his side.
Then the disciples rejoiced when they saw the Lord. Jesus said to
them again, "Peace be with you. As the Father has sent me, so
I send you." When he had said this, he breathed on them and
said to them, "Receive the Holy Spirit. If you forgive the sins of
any, they are forgiven them; if you retain the sins of any, they
are retained."
(John 20:19-23 NRSV)

An Incarnational Commission

John's Gospel is different than the other Gospels in many respects, and
this is the case regarding the commission of the risen Jesus to his disciples. In all three Synoptic Gospels, the commission of Jesus is verbal. In
John, Jesus' commission is *incarnational:* "As the Father has sent me, so
I send you."

Some point out that this doesn't seem very helpful. Matthew, Mark,
and Luke all focus on *why* the disciples are *sent*—to make disciples of
Christ, to teach and baptize, to bear witness to him, to proclaim repentance and forgiveness, and so on. But John doesn't specify anything at
all, they say, making the commission vague and imprecise. But not so.
Incarnation isn't a quirk of the commission of Christ in John but is a
key theme of that Gospel. John's Gospel opens with that great prologue
about the Word. *The Word that became flesh and dwelt among us in Christ.*
The commission of Jesus in John's Gospel is, in effect, to be like Jesus.
Lesslie Newbigin taught and wrote often about embodied mission being
the best mission of all, because it follows the pattern of incarnation. He
used to say that every word in the sentence, "As the Father has sent me, so
I send you," was important, but that the most important word was "as."[3]

---

[3] Lesslie Newbigin, see his Commentary on John's Gospel, *The
Light Has Come: An Exposition of the Fourth Gospel* (Grand Rapids, MI:

As Jesus was, may you be. As Jesus did it, do it like that. Be like him. Because, Newbigin said, the very heart of Christian mission is being like Jesus. As he was *sent*, we are *sent*. There's nothing vague about that.

The yearnings of a congregation to be more profoundly mission-shaped and committed to authentic and appropriate evangelism almost always arise from an incarnational impulse, a deep desire to be with people, and often people not found in any church and professing no firm religious beliefs at all. It is a yearning to create communities of mutual respect, safety, care, and trust, healthy contexts in which Christian faith can be shared and owned, and life in all its fullness lived out. Such churches tend to keep it pretty simple. They eat together, talk together, pray together, and relax and work together with others for kingdom causes. Fresh expressions doesn't invite people to come to church as much as to become church among people. Like the disciples to whom the risen Jesus appears, Fresh Expression communities know that Christianity cannot be properly incarnational when kept behind closed doors.

In all four Gospels, but particularly here in John, the risen Christ comes to disciples with mission far from their minds. Being locked away in a room is a poignant antitype of mission. Then Jesus stands among them, and everything changes. They meet the risen Jesus, who shows them his pierced hands and side. But they know too that they're in the presence of the divine Christ, who comes through locked doors, the Living One who died. It is Jesus Christ, both human and divine, who commissions them. From that time on, they are moving outwards. They are *sent*.

Pause...

What do you think would be involved for your local church to become more incarnational?

How do you think your own discipleship of Christ could become more sent as Christ was sent?

Wm. B. Eerdmans, 1982) as well as his *The Gospel in a Pluralist Society* (Grand Rapids, MI: 1986).

Another impulse that helps create fresh expressions is a new or renewed sense of meeting Jesus. At one time the renewing of faith in an individual or congregation would have usually resulted in increased or more regular attendance at Sunday worship, or the beginning of a new prayer meeting or project. Increasingly today, when people meet Jesus anew, they feel led outwards. *Sent.* Some feel led to become missionaries around the world. Many more feel God's call to represent and embody Jesus their Lord among those much nearer to home, to stand with and among those who do not yet know Christ and together become church in new ways. They are *sent.*

There's a natural tension in incarnation, and that arises in large part from its relationship with the world. We see the tension in the way John 1:14 is sometimes translated. One paraphrase states that "the Word became flesh and blood and moved into the neighborhood." The Divine Word becomes a human being. God, in Christ, makes his home in the world. So how can his church do otherwise? But another paraphrase translation of John 1:14 states that "the Word became flesh and tabernacled among us." The tabernacle in the Old Testament was the portable earthly dwelling place of God, carried from place to place by the people of Israel, as in the words of the spiritual song, "this world is not my home, I'm just passin' through." For Christians, earth, for all its wonder and beauty, is a temporary dwelling place. That is why St. Paul refers to our bodies as tents and tells us that our true citizenship lies in heaven. Ultimately, the kingdom of God is not of this world, and neither the Christian church nor Christ's disciples must make it so.

All Christians and their congregations recognize and live with the inherent tension of being incarnational. But those who seek to become more fully mission-shaped and birth fresh expressions tend not to adopt a distant or opt-out stance in relation to the world. They are very aware that the world is not the same as God's kingdom and are not naïve about evil forces in it. But essentially, they understand the world as a place of people loved by God, and they understand the church as God's agency of love to the world. They live out their life and witness as Jesus' disciples, aware that ultimately the world God loves—and in Christ died to save—cannot be saved or served by dis-incarnation. In short, they tend to opt-in and get dirty fingernails rather than opt-out and stay pristine and unmarked. In John's Gospel, whenever the word *apostellein* (meaning sent out) is used, the apostles are being *sent* into the world.

> Pause...
>
> *In what ways does your church opt-out or opt-in in relation to embodying Jesus Christ in the world?*
>
> *How do you think the message of this section relates to the old saying that "Christians should be in the world but not of it?"*

The Easter Spirit

Unlike Luke, who records a fifty day period between Christ's resurrection and the Day of Pentecost, which includes Jesus' ascension into heaven, John's Pentecost takes place on the evening of the first Easter Day.

There's no mention of Luke's wind, flames, and doves, but John does employ another deeply evocative and rich biblical image. He tells us the risen Jesus *breathes* on his disciples. Now, when you are reading John's Gospel prologue, it's good to have the book of Genesis in mind. Genesis begins with the words, "In the beginning God," and it's no accident that John's Gospel begins "In the beginning was the Word." Here "Creation" and "New Creation in Christ" both mean God's Word. Remember how in one of the Genesis stories of creation God takes the dust of the earth and forms it? But it isn't truly human, isn't a living soul, until God breathes life into it. Or, for all lovers of the Narnia chronicles by C. S. Lewis, remember how Aslan (the Christ-lion) restores all those that have been petrified by the White Witch in a time when it's always winter and never Christmas? He *breathes* on them. *"Peace be with you,"* Jesus says, twice, for emphasis. "As the Father has sent me, so I send you." Then he *breathes* on them and says, "Receive the Holy Spirit." It's John's Pentecost. The bestowing of the Spirit is inextricably linked to going, to being sent, sent like Jesus, sent to be like Jesus, sent in the power of the Spirit.

In the commissioning of Christ in Matthew and Luke, the Holy Spirit is understood mainly as power given to fulfil it. That is also true of John's Gospel, but other richer roles of the Spirit are also identified. The Spirit is the *Paraclete* (one alongside), helper, comforter, advocate, intercessor, and mediator to those who know and follow Christ. The Spirit teaches, guides, and abides. In terms of the world, the Spirit reveals and glorifies Christ, convinces, convicts, illuminates, and judges. In John, it is the Holy Spirit of all these rich roles that is breathed into the first disciples, and disciples ever since. Including us. We are sent to go as Jesus was sent, enabled by the Holy Spirit to be Jesus in a world where Christ and Christlikeness remain so much needed.

Pause...

Have you any experiences of being breathed into by God's Holy Spirit?

How many of the roles of the Holy Spirit do you recognize as present and active in you and in the life of your local church?

Mission-shaped churches and fresh expressions take very seriously the notion of incarnating and embodying the Christ they follow and the gospel they proclaim. Indeed, in almost all books about fresh expressions (what they are, why they begin, and how they work) the commitment to incarnational mission and ministry is emphatic. We note how very attractive being like Jesus is, and how when we experience or encounter authentic incarnation, it moves us. Both mission-shaped churches and fresh expressions tend (almost instinctively) not to regard themselves as salespeople or even advocates of Christianity as much as free gifts and samples of God's love in Christ.

Summary

In this chapter, we've sought to offer evidence to support the assertion that there is what Arias called a Great Commission of Jesus found in each Gospel. Also, that rather than being proof texts, potentially disconnected from the overall content of that Gospel, these are in fact, in each case, accurately illustrative of the commission of Christ found throughout the gospel. We don't regard these as the most important things, however. Two things are more significant. First is that this material supports our deep conviction that the gospels are, in their entirety, missiological in nature, and as such *together* offer a broader, more wonderful and challenging commission of Jesus than any single Gospel does or can. Second, that in recognizing and accepting the worth of these broader mission themes, churches desirous of being more mission-shaped and fertile with apt evangelism and fresh expressions can discover that both the *missio Dei* and Great Commission understandings of mission are required to be understood, explored, and applied in order to be so.

Peter and Paul: Conversion and Call

It is an understatement to say that Peter and Paul have had an enormous influence upon the Christian movement throughout the world: from the origins of the Eastern and Western Church, to the translation of the gospel into almost every language and culture, to the role of women in leadership.

Peter and Paul are both exemplary and flawed: we look up to them as role models in the faith, and yet we have our issues with them. In the New Testament—and much of the New Testament is shaped by these two apostles—Peter and Paul are portrayed as very human figures. Nothing is glossed over. They are real flesh and blood people, just like we are.

In reflecting on two passages that are pivotal for Peter and Paul, we might describe these as their conversion or their call experiences. Within the two passages, we can see similarities and differences. Our hope is that within these two passages, we will each and all discover something about ourselves, about our own need for conversion, and about our own callings.

(Read John 21: 1-19 at this point.)

First Peter. The risen Jesus has appeared on the beach to the disciples. They share a meal (in this case breakfast) of bread and fish. We find rich symbolism here: we think of the feeding of the five thousand, of Jesus' own statement that he is the Bread of Life, and of his first call to them to fish for men and women.

After the meal, Jesus and Peter are in conversation. Jesus asks Peter the same question three times: "Do you love me?" And three times Peter responds, "Yes, Lord, I love you." Then three times Jesus gives a command: "Feed my sheep (tend my lambs)." Many in the early Christian community heard in those three questions and three responses an echo of the three denials of Christ by Peter at his arrest. In fact, many interpreters see the account in John 21 as the early church's response to the question, "What happened to Peter? How was Peter restored?" The one who denied that he knew Christ, who fled when it became too difficult and dangerous and disturbing, is now in a face-to-face conversation with Jesus.

It is a conversation that has to do with conversion and call. The conversion is about what Jesus wants Peter to do, about what will be required of Peter. The one who said "I am the Good Shepherd" is now calling upon Peter to feed his sheep, to care for the Christian community, and to love others. And yet, this caring will be costly. Peter will stretch out his arms in suffering, and the one who is the leader will be led to places that he would rather not go. The way of the cross for Jesus will become the way of the cross, for Peter. After this, Jesus says simply, "Follow me."

Pause . . .

Is the love of Christ still at the heart of your discipleship, or if not, what is?

(Read Acts 9:1-19 at this point.)

We shift our focus now from Peter to Paul, although early in the story his name is Saul. Saul is on the way to Syria on the Damascus Road. Saul was prominent among the persecutors of the earliest Christians. Luke tells us that he was present when Stephen was martyred. Along the way, Saul is struck by lightning, is blinded, and hears a voice: "Saul, Saul, why do you persecute me?" Saul responds, "Who are you, Lord?" The response: "I am Jesus, whom you are persecuting."

This incident is so important that it is told three times in the book of Acts, getting more detailed at points with each telling, like a family story that we keep repeating because of its profound significance. We must not miss the fact that Saul's persecution of believers in Christ is regarded by Christ as persecution of himself, which has profound implications for our treatment of one another within the Body of Christ.

God uses Ananias to interpret what is happening to Paul. Ananias receives a message, an impulse from God that he should go to Saul and lay hands on him so that he might receive his sight. Ananias' immediate response is understandable: "Lord, how can I reach out to this person? He's a threat to us. He has been complicit in the murder of our people."

We sometimes feel an impulse to reach out to people beyond the church, don't we? Maybe we invite them to be a part of what God is doing in God's church. Perhaps we invite them to be a part of a small group or to attend a worship service. Other times, we hold back. What keeps us from reaching out? "He might be offended. She might not respond. He is too busy. They might reject me." We can think of many reasons for not getting involved in someone else's life, even when we feel an impulse to do so.

Ananias has a wonderful excuse. Saul is the enemy, and he's danger-ous. But God simply says, "Go, for he will be my instrument to take the gospel to the Gentiles, and, by the way, he will experience great suffering along the way." The way of the cross for Jesus will become the way of the cross for Paul. Ananias listens and responds. He intervenes, and he goes to Saul. Note what happens. He goes into the house of Saul, he lays hands on him, and says, "Brother Saul."

He includes Saul as his brother before Saul ever says a word. That is evangelism. We sometimes think evangelism is about how the other person will respond, but it really begins with us. What if we imagined that the person that we are being sent to is already our brother or our sister? Saul is radically different from Ananias, yet Ananias already knows that he is his brother in Christ. He is already a part of the family.

Saul's sight is restored. He was blind, but now he sees. He is baptized, he eats, and he regains his strength.

> Pause . . .
>
> Do you have impulses to go talk to someone? What do you usually do about them?
>
> To what extent does your congregation count someone as part of the family before they've said a word?

These are the formative experiences of conversion and call in the lives of Peter and Paul. To Peter, conversion is coming face to face with the compassionate, forgiving shepherd who loves him, and whom he is invited to love and follow. For Paul, conversion is a blinding flash of insight, seeing the whole world in a new way. For Peter, conversion is a reminder of much that he had been taught over a period of time. For Paul, conversion is a radically new orientation in life. For Peter, call is all about becoming more compassionate and sharing the love of God with those in the household of faith. For Paul, call is all about going into the world and sharing the grace of God with those who are outside the household of faith. Peter is the shepherd whose ministry is used by God to also be an evangelist. Paul is the evangelist whose ministry is used by God to also be a shepherd. Peter's focus is largely internal. Paul's focus is largely external. Later, in Acts 15 and also in Galatians, their two callings sometimes come into uneasy conflict. They each meet the risen Lord, but their experiences of conversion and call are very different. They are very real, but very different.

Now what does all of this mean for us? Most of us do not encounter a flash of lightning in the sky or hear an audible voice. Yet, conversions still happen. So, what about our own experience of the risen Christ and our own sense of how, where, and to what Jesus is calling us?

An acquaintance of a friend of Ken's loved working with old cars and was obsessed with one in particular: a Mustang. He purchased the Mustang and began the laborious process of transforming it back to its original condition. There were really two steps in the process: first to rescue the car, then to restore the car. The restoration was a long, involved process, because it included scraping away all the rust before the painting could begin.

In Jesus Christ, we have been rescued. God does not give up on Peter, or Paul, or you, or me. The cross is the sign of God's desire to rescue us, even when our pasts haunt us, even when we have been at odds with all that God represents. But we experience more than rescue. We also receive restoration. Every person is created in the image of God, in the image of a God who is love, in the image of a God who loves the world so much that he gave up his Son. This is a slow and laborious process of restoration. It is the painful conversation between Peter and Jesus, or the blinding reorientation of Paul on the road to Damascus.

Conversion is not watching a television program or hearing a preacher then settling it all in a few minutes and moving on. Conversion is a lifelong process of being restored into a relationship with the One who created us in the first place. A part of that conversion is the call to give our lives for some purpose. Here again, call takes on different forms.

For Peter, the call is essentially to take care of the sheep. For Paul, the call is essentially to share the gospel with the Gentiles. What is your call? In our experience, the call can take on a diversity of expressions. That's the beauty of the Christian community. One is called to sing. One is called to be a Stephen Minister. One is called to give medical care in

Haiti. One is called to spend the night with the homeless. One is called to befriend a middle school boy or girl. One is called to teach. One is called to make the church more welcoming to gays and lesbians. One is called to share the catechism that he learned as a child with confirmands. One is called to teach the Bible in prison. One is called to practice hospitality to a family in grief. One is called to support the church financially. One is called to love adults with disabilities. One is called to be an advocate with people suffering from Multiple Sclerosis. One is called to befriend foreign missionaries.

Not until a congregation of Christ's people realize that every member is called (not just the commissioned or ordained) and begin to exercise that call in obedience to Christ and the ministry of the church, does a church become more mission-shaped.

Pause...

How do you define your call?

What is the evidence of continuing conversion and restoration in your local church?

God always calls imperfect people, like Peter and Paul, like you and me. The way of the cross for Jesus will become the way of the cross for you and me. Call will at times involve suffering. Call will lead us to places we had not imagined ourselves going. Our callings will take different forms, as different as our life stories.

Ken writes:

I want to briefly share some of my own experience of conversion and call. It began in the midst of a difficult adolescence, partly due to changes within our family, partly the result of racial turmoil in our Deep South community, partly due to normal teenage confusion. There were changes in our family, changes in the schools (due to integration and busing), and changes in my home church, which always seemed to be in some kind of crisis. In those years, everything that was settled became unsettled. It was by the grace of God that I survived those years. I was a pretty self-absorbed teenager, and I did not have the benefit of a good youth ministry.

As I began college, I joined a fraternity. In short, life became pretty excessive, as you might imagine. At some point, I realized that all of this was not leading to a good place, and I was not becoming a person that I liked very much, although I did not give it a great deal of deep thought. And so, I resigned from the fraternity, as quietly as possible.

For some reason, I found my way to a campus ministry group. Over time, something began to happen. I was an outsider at first, but along the way, the church became a home. Later, I talked about all of this with the pastor of my church, whom I had never really known. Just the idea of sitting down and talking with a preacher was something I had never imagined myself doing! No audible voices, no blinding flashes of light, but it was a turning point. I embraced this faith as my own. Something had been salvaged.

In time, my conversion became a call. I began to try to integrate what this meant in my life. My studies shifted from biology to psychology to theology. I began to explore the call: what would I do with my life? I have lived long enough to be able to look back on some of it all and gain perspective. I can only say that for me, the call has been and is still to the church—to Christ's wonderful, diverse, frustrating, challenging church.

There is much about life in the church that neither you nor I can control. There are no set office hours. We don't go home at 5:00 p.m. We don't give people grades. We relate to anyone who walks through the doors. It is somewhat unpredictable. The local church is not perfect, but the local church is real. It is where Christ is—a place where he can be found and still is found. As surely as Peter has a call and Paul has a call, this is my call. It is like a salvaged car in that there is a lot of rust to be scraped away, but at times the light shines through, and God's grace is visible.

Pause...

Is your locale a place where Christ can be found and still is found?

Is your church a place where diverse people experience conversion and call?

If so—or if not—where is God leading you next in order that you might be a more useful vessel for God's mission?

The Holy Spirit of Mission: Three Studies in Acts

The Acts or just Acts. That's how the fifth book of the New Testament is most commonly known. Whose Acts? The Acts of the Apostles of course. That's the full title found in all Bibles for many hundreds of years. Yet, as has been pointed out repeatedly over Christian history, the book more accurately tells of the Acts of the Holy Spirit of God. For those committed to creating mission-shaped churches and multiple types of fresh expressions pregnant with reimagined evangelism (as we are) this produces some important convictions. First, the Acts of the Apostles makes clear that the Holy Spirit, the third Person of the Holy Trinity, is the God of mission, on mission, and the enabler of that which Christ commands. Second and consequentially, the Holy Spirit in Acts always leads the way. It is the prime mover. The believers don't always immediately discern the leading of the Spirit, but they are always responding to God's mission rather than initiating it. Therefore, third: from the very beginning, believers in Jesus Christ were invited or commanded to be on mission with the Holy Spirit. They are not spectators, but Spirit-filled and Spirit-led partners and participants in what the God of mission is doing. The more they experience

and learn of the Holy Spirit of mission, the more useful they are in participating in the commission of Christ and the deep and wonderful purposes
of the *missio Dei.*

For a long time, the book of Acts was thought to be mostly a type
of history book. While it's true that the writer (thought by most scholars
to be the same evangelist who wrote Luke's Gospel) includes all sorts
of names, dates, and places, Acts is not *primarily* a historical account.
Essentially, it records the activity of a missionary God seen supremely
in terms of Holy Spirit. Consequently, unless we understand Acts to be
a book of Spirit and mission, we won't accurately understand its primary
purpose. Luke's doctrine of the Holy Spirit—to use a technical phrase,
his *pneumatology*—is fundamentally missiological. St. John and St. Paul's
writings both focus more on the saving function of the Spirit and the
beingness of the Spirit in the Holy Trinity of God. Luke doesn't dispute
any of this, but his deepest interest in Acts is the Holy Spirit of God who
empowers and directs the earliest believers in Christ to pursue Christ's
commission and participate in the mission of God.

It's said that during World War II, as Russian soldiers retreated over
frozen ground, they could be seen carrying water faucets attached to a
couple of feet of pipe in their rucksacks. They carried these, believing that
wherever they were, they could simply place the pipe on the ground, turn
the tap, and water would flow. Apparently, the hard-frozen road verges
were strewn with taps and piping as they offloaded useless weight. In our
life together in church, whenever we try to separate Spirit from mission,
mission from Spirit, we attempt to divorce what God intends to be indis-
solubly interrelated. Or, put more positively, because the Spirit of God is
essentially the Spirit of mission, whenever Christ's church is engaged in
God's mission and good evangelism as a vital part of it, it can be assured
that it is filled and resourced with the Holy Spirit.

What follows are three studies, or reflections from the Acts of the
Apostles. As in our earlier reflections on the Gospels and the calls of
Peter and Paul, comments about the text are interspersed with attempts
to apply mission themes to the life of the church. Some of these mission
themes connect and overlap with others made elsewhere in this book,

while others don't. Through these studies—as with the whole of this book—we seek to encourage a greater participation in God's mission, a renewed commitment to the commission of Christ, resulting in more and better mission-shaped churches, appropriate and reimagined evangelism, and a rich variety of fresh expressions.

The Day of Pentecost (Acts 2:1-14)

Where better to start than the world-transforming event known as the Day of Pentecost?

> When the day of Pentecost had come, they were all together in one place. And suddenly from heaven there came a sound like the rush of a violent wind, and it filled the entire house where they were sitting. Divided tongues, as of fire, appeared among them, and a tongue rested on each of them. All of them were filled with the Holy Spirit and began to speak in other languages, as the Spirit gave them ability.
>
> Now there were devout Jews from every nation under heaven living in Jerusalem. And at this sound the crowd gathered and was bewildered, because each one heard them speaking in the native language of each. Amazed and astonished, they asked, "Are not all these who are speaking Galileans? And how is it that we hear, each of us, in our own native language? Parthians, Medes, Elamites, and residents of Mesopotamia, Judea and Cappadocia, Pontus and Asia, Phrygia and Pamphylia, Egypt and the parts of Libya belonging to Cyrene, and visitors from Rome, both Jews and proselytes, Cretans and Arabs—in our own languages we hear them speaking about God's deeds of power." All were amazed and perplexed, saying to one another, "What does this mean?" But others sneered and said, "They are filled with new wine."
>
> But Peter, standing with the eleven, raised his voice and addressed them.—Acts 2:1-14 NRSV

Resonances, Signals, and Clues

We understand this passage better when we remember that what Christians call Pentecost was already a long-established Jewish festival. That's why Jerusalem is filled with Jews from around the known world. It was expected of devout Jews that they would make the pilgrimage to Jerusalem for this festival—the Feast of Weeks—at least once in their lives, much like Muslims are expected to make Hajjchris to Mecca. By the time of Jesus, the Jewish festival was associated with several themes that resonate with what is recorded as happening here at the first Christian Pentecost.

For example, the Feast of Weeks remembered and celebrated God's giving of the Law to Moses. The story was well known by all Jews. At this crucial event on Mount Sinai, when the presence and instructions of God were made known—God of whom no images could be made or whose form clearly seen—fire and cloudy wind marked the occasion. Nor was this an isolated association. God used a burning bush that was not consumed to call Moses and led the people of Israel out of slavery in Egypt by a pillar of fire. Wind was also associated with divine presence and action. Both the original Hebrew and Greek words for Spirit can be translated wind or breath, and Jews knew that the Spirit blew over the waters at the beginning of creation, just as in another story of creation God breathed life into the dust of the earth causing it to become human living souls. So, on that Pentecost day when wind comes and fire falls on the believers, and they burst into the streets speaking everyone's languages, there's some confusion to be sure, but the clues are clear. God is present in power and is making known something important.

The Jewish festival was also a time for renewing covenant with God, the covenant made by the giving of the Law through Moses and again through Jeremiah—the law written in human hearts rather than on stone. So, when Peter stands up and begins to interpret the new thing God is doing, which the crowd is witnessing, and appeals to them to turn again to God in penitence, there's some confusion, but the clues and signals would resonate with many hearers. This is a time of the renewal of faith.

Alongside this older theme of renewal was a more recent belief that the Feast of Weeks was a time when Messiah might come. Or as Joel and other later Old Testament prophets put it, a time when God's Spirit would be poured out on both men *and* women, the enemies of Israel would be routed, and God's people given privilege and power. So, when the Holy Spirit falls upon the (Jewish) believers, it confuses but also sends signals and gives clues. Is this the year? Is this when Messiah comes?

Perhaps most well-known, the Jewish Pentecost was a kind of harvest festival. A sheaf of barley was offered to God as part of the Passover feast, the first fruits of an early harvest. Then, fifty days later came the Feast of Weeks, which included the offering to God of the first fruits of the wheat harvest. So, when three thousand people become believers that first Christian Pentecost—the harvest, the first fruits of this moving of God's Spirit—there are clues and signals, the meaning of which could and would be discerned.

It's important to remember that the disciples and other believers in Christ gathered in Jerusalem on that Day of Pentecost are all Jews. Like all other Jews, they know the traditions, hopes, and expectations associated with the Feast. Also, and uniquely, they are deeply aware that they have been told by the risen Jesus, just before he returned to his Father in heaven, to wait in Jerusalem where they will receive the promised Holy Spirit. So here they are, fearful but obedient, and acutely aware of signals of meaning as the momentous events of the day unfold.

The Outward Urge

One more theme must be noted which is particularly significant to those seeking to create mission-shaped churches and fresh expressions. In the context of this Law-remembering, covenant-renewing, God-revealing, Messiah-anticipating, first-fruits-celebrating Pentecost festival, there had grown up a close association with the city of Jerusalem. The significance of Jerusalem in Jewish faith is asserted repeatedly in the Old Testament. It's the city of God on a hill. It's a light to the nations, because a prominent belief was that the (unbelieving) nations from north, south, east, and west would one day come to Jerusalem. There were different opinions about how the nations would come. Some said they would come reluctantly and in chains, would be judged, and done away with. Others said the nations of the world would come to see the light, realize the Jews were indeed the chosen people of the One True God, cast off their sub-standard religions, and come rejoicing into holy Jerusalem—Zion, the city of our God. So as Jews came to Jerusalem to celebrate their Pentecost, there was expectancy which would only be heightened when the events recorded in Acts 2 took place. Is this the year when God restores Jerusalem to Israel? Is this the time when the nations will come and pay homage to our God, the One True God?

When the Spirit comes, however, instead of everything being drawn to Jerusalem, things immediately begin to move outwards not inwards: "You shall receive power when the Holy Spirit comes upon you," Jesus tells the disciples, "and you will be my witnesses in Jerusalem, in all Judea and Samaria, and to the ends of the earth." The great New Testament scholar F. F. Bruce used to say of the book of Acts: "It is as if God drops a pebble into the pool of human history, and you watch the ripples."[4] The centripetal Pentecost of the Jewish tradition is replaced by a centrifugal Christian Pentecost. Christianity is, from the beginning, an outwards faith, because God—Father, Son, and Holy Spirit—is the God of mission.

This outwards urge is very important to those of us committed to creating mission-shaped churches, fresh expressions, and reimagined evangelism, and leads to a fundamental conviction. If the nature of God is missionary, how can the nature of the church—that owes its very existence to God, who in Christ died to redeem it and by the Spirit seeks to lead it, fill it, and use it—be anything other or different? So, in this text in Acts 2, we witness a radical change in the believers when the Spirit comes. At first, there they are, like so many local churches are, apprehensively living behind closed doors, outside of which is a world of clamor and crisis, wonder and challenge, opportunity and need.

---

[4] F. F. Bruce, from his lectures at the University of Manchester where Martyn did his initial College training as a Methodist pastor.

We must note here what we *don't* read in the text. We don't read that the Holy Spirit falls upon the believers, and they remain in the room to have a charismatic prayer meeting. Now, for fear of being misunderstood, we must make it clear that we are decidedly for prayer meetings. But we recognize the fact that a deep experience of the Holy Spirit doesn't automatically propel Christians outwards. We've all encountered very content holy huddles—often very nice, if somewhat hard to join. So, we notice that here and throughout the Acts, the presence of the Holy Spirit always produces movement, and the movement is invariably outwards, toward others. We also don't read that the Holy Spirit falls on the believers, who then engage in a long and heated debate about whether now is the right time for a revival. We don't read that they conclude, by a small majority, that they ought to have a mission and duly set up a committee to decide what it shall be like and when it shall be. Nor, finally, do we read that they subsequently decide to postpone the mission until they get the room properly decorated and arrange that everyone is better trained to deal with all manner of questions that just might conceivably be posed to them!

Instead, the Holy Spirit of God who comes at Pentecost impels the believers in Jesus *onto* the streets. In fact, the Spirit comes both *inside and outside* that room, and the believers and the crowd alike are caught up in that divine activity and must quickly make a crucial choice. Do we resist the Spirit or go with the Spirit? Because ultimately, being mission-shaped isn't merely something you do, it's something you *are,* because you belong to the God of mission.

Pause . . .

To what extent do you think and act as if the Holy Spirit is the Spirit of mission?

Do you regard your local church as a centrifugal or a centripetal community?

The Direction of Holiness

In which direction is holiness found? It's a strange but significant question in terms of the nature of God's mission and one this Pentecost text engages.

Holiness is often assumed to be inwards, which is not wholly wrong but not completely right. Through the years, both of us have heard a prayer offered in the vestry as we prepare to walk into the sanctuary to lead worship that goes something like this: "We thank you Lord that we can come apart from the world and draw near to you in your house for this holy hour. . . ." Holiness is often associated with withdrawal from the world. Holiness guards itself from corruption and temptation. It keeps its distance. It keeps itself pure. It is above and apart. We sometimes see this attitude in the Pharisees and their dividing of the whole of life into a clean-unclean dualism. As a result, they stand apart from others and express holiness by scrupulous adherence to numerous outward rituals, which is, of course, criticized hotly and repeatedly by Jesus who makes clear three things. First that the pursuit of holiness is good and right— "Be perfect, as your heavenly Father is perfect." Second, that holiness is essentially what is inside a person rather than mere outward show—"Woe to you, hypocrites! You clean the outside of the cup and dish but inside are full of greed." Third, that holiness necessarily works itself out by true and proper actions—"So when you give something to a needy person do not make a big show of it."

It's vital to recognize therefore that on the Day of Pentecost it is the *Holy* Spirit who fills the believers in Jesus Christ and impels, leads, and accompanies them *out* of the room, *onto* the streets, and *into* the world. The Holy Spirit is not merely the title or name of the Third Person of the Trinity. *Holiness* is her very nature, and it is a sent and sending holiness, not just here in Jerusalem at Pentecost but repeatedly in Acts: through Philip in the Desert, Peter at the house of Cornelius, Paul in . . . well, most everywhere! Fundamentally holiness understood as remote and apart is not easily compatible with participating in the mission of God. We find ourselves a little too far away from where the Holy Spirit is. In a profoundly incarnated faith like Christianity, mission by megaphone has little to commend it, in terms of either theology or practice.

In an earlier ministry, Martyn taught religious studies to teenaged schoolchildren and asked them to name some holy people. One name always came up in the first couple of suggestions: Mother Teresa of Calcutta. You know, that well-known recluse, who never soiled her hands with the sins of the world? No! A woman bent—quite literally—towards serving the poorest people amid squalor and dirt, yet somehow recognized as being holy. This is probably because she reminds us of Jesus, who seemed to attract sinners like a magnet and yet was the Holy One. Christian holiness is holiness with dirty fingernails. It is essentially opting in, not out. Its direction is both inwards *and* outwards. It is about being filled and sent by a Holy God.

> *Pause...*
>
> *Talk about your experiences of holiness and holy people. Were they inwardly holy, outwardly holy, or both?*
>
> *In what ways does your church exhibit holiness with dirty fingernails?*

Tongues and All That

What's the main purpose of the gift of tongues in this text?

Martyn recalls:

> My Christian life began in the early 1970s, a time of charismatic renewal in many churches, including mine. Speaking in tongues, the gifts of the Spirit, and all that was a big issue when I was seventeen. I remember the holy thrill when you spoke aloud in a tongue language you didn't know and the sense of being used of God as someone interpreted the tongue to the gathered group. Writers wrote books about the renewing of the Holy Spirit, and I read them avidly. Certain churches became centers of pilgrimage for blessing, and like many others, I went along to see what was happening. The gifts of the Spirit were often explained to

be gifts to the church to build up the Body of Christ, to make it strong and holy. Now, several decades later, I'm not disowning any of it. It was an exciting time of real spiritual growth for me, and—praise God—I'm still zapped by the Holy Spirit from time to time! But I came to regard it all as a little too inward-looking, too comfortable. More seriously, it defined my understanding of the Holy Spirit. I acted and assumed as if the Spirit of God were merely the blesser-up of the church, and me as part of it. At worst, I sometimes treated the Holy Spirit a bit like a vending machine: "I've prayed fervently for more gifts Lord; where are they?" Without suggesting for a moment that the Spirit doesn't bless and strengthen the church, particularly when it is persecuted, I came to understand this view of the Holy Spirit as inadequate, too small, reduced, and domesticated. I like to think it was the Holy Spirit herself who helped me along this road!

It was this Pentecost passage that helped me in this growth point on my spiritual journey of mission-shaped mindedness and the pursuit of good, reimagined evangelism and fresh expressions. It both intrigued and stretched me. The Holy Spirit falls on the believers, and they began to speak in other languages—tongues given by the Spirit. I understood this. It had happened to me. But as I read on, cracks in my assumptions began to appear. The text made clear that the most significant thing about the gift of tongues wasn't what I expected. It wasn't the spiritual blessing of the believers receiving this gift of the Spirit, though I'm sure it was a wonderful experience. It wasn't the building up of the church, though it's fantastic that we go on to read that three thousand people joined the community of believers that day. No, the essential purpose of the gift of tongues on the Day of Pentecost was this: People from all over the known world understood what the believers were saying: "How is it that we hear, each of us, in our own native language?" they ask, astonished. This is the miracle: that they all heard the praises of God and the proclamation about Jesus Christ in their own tongues. Speakers of dozens of dialects and tens of mother tongues all say, in effect, "they're speaking my language!" The Pentecost gift enabled those who needed to hear the gospel to do so. It was, unsurprisingly, profoundly evangelistic in nature and purpose.

Those of us committed to mission-shaped church and fresh expressions regard this as significant. It's not a once off, but rather illustrates an essential truth about the nature of God. God is a God of mission and from the beginning empowers and co-opts believers in Christ to make Christ known in word and deed.

Pause...

How do you respond to Martyn's testimony about understanding the role and purpose of the Holy Spirit?

Share with others how your own understanding of some aspect of Christian faith has evolved over time?

Translatability

Have you ever thought that the Holy Spirit of God could have chosen to do this miracle of tongues another way? Instead of enabling each person in Jerusalem to hear the gospel through the believers in their own language, she could have performed a different miracle. God could have instantly taught everyone present a single, common language. Then everyone would have only had to learn one. It would be a kind of ecstatic Esperanto. You know, Esperanto . . . the universal language invented in the 1880s spoken by . . . well, not many people at all really! And that's the point. God didn't choose the Esperanto route. The God of mission knows that for the gospel to be truly good news, you need to hear it in your own language.

In his book *Translating the Message* and other places, the late Professor of Missions at Yale Divinity School, Lamin Sanneh, talks about the genius of Christianity being its translatability. Raised in a Muslim household in The Gambia in West Africa and later converting to Christianity, he sensitively contrasted how Islam and Christianity learn and share their holy scriptures. Whereas Islam urges that Muslims everywhere do best to learn to read the Qur'an in its native classical Arabic, Christianity has historically adopted the principle of translation much more extensively. The translation of the Bible and particularly the Gospels has been a key component of Christian mission since the early centuries CE. That's not surprising given the wealth of evidence for the evangelistic effectiveness of reading the Bible in your own language or dialect.

Those committed to reimagined evangelism and mission-shaped, fresh expressions of church are deeply committed to translatability, not only the formal translating of scripture, which is a highly skilled calling, but also and particularly to lessening the distances between the life of the local Christian church—its vocabulary, worship, cultures, and body language, as well as those of the peoples and populations living and working in the neighborhood. For mission-minded folk, this is more important than creating a local church for themselves or running it how they would ideally like it. They're profoundly affected by the disturbing reality that many of their friends and relatives make plain in various ways that "what goes on in church bears no relationship to my life at all." Therefore, fresh expressions of church are often characterized by sacrifice rather than a selfishness of which they are sometimes accused. Almost instinctively, they're aware that God always rejects the Esperanto route and so regard the Pentecost miracle as confirmation that the Holy Spirit prefers variety. God's intention for the church of Christ then cannot be a monochrome, mono-cultural, mono-lingual organization but a vibrant, diverse community. Under and beyond all these convictions and instincts is an awareness, not always explicitly articulated but always cherished, that God in Christ led the way in the most profound translatability known as incarnation.

Pause...

What would it mean for your congregation to make a deeper commitment to translatability?

What do you think are the most significant insights from this study for you and your local church?

Peter and Cornelius (Acts 10)

The story of the Apostle Peter and a Roman centurion called Cornelius is told in Acts 10:1-48. It's a long story and isn't reproduced in full here, though we offer an outline of it below. However, it will be helpful to read the full text before reading on, so you might want to do that now.

Though the story is long (and some writers suggest that its length indicates the high significance it has for Luke and the early church communities who knew this story), the basic plot is relatively simple. Cornelius is a high-ranking Roman and a God-fearing man. An angel of God appears to him telling him to send for a stranger, a man called Simon Peter, who is in Joppa. So, he does. Before they meet, the narrative moves to Peter who has a vision. A blanket, full of animals and birds including those that Jewish law states are unclean and therefore mustn't be eaten, comes down from heaven. "Kill and eat these," God says. Peter refuses, pointing out they're unclean. "What God makes clean you mustn't call unclean," the voice replies, but Peter still refuses, three times in all, and the food disappears into heaven. At this point, the servants of Cornelius arrive to ask Peter to go with them, while at the same time, the Spirit is telling Peter he must agree to go. The next day, a group set off together to Cornelius' home. On arrival, many people are assembled, and Cornelius, deeply respectful, asks Peter to enter and speak. Peter points out that it's against Jewish law for him to associate with a Gentile but that, crucially, God has shown him that he mustn't call anyone unclean, and asks what Cornelius wants of him. The story of Cornelius' visit by an angel is recounted, and Peter becomes aware that it is God's will that he shares the gospel with the gathered Gentiles. "I realize now that God shows no partiality, has no favorites," Peter says. "Anyone who fears God and does what is right is acceptable to God," and he proceeds to bear witness to Jesus, telling of his life, death and resurrection. Before Peter finishes speaking, the Holy Spirit falls on the whole gathering, and they begin to praise God in tongues. Peter is astounded but recognizes this as God's blessing and acceptance of Gentiles, and he insists that they be baptized in the name of Christ. He stays with them a few days.

Locating the Story

It's hard to imagine the amount of change and transition going on in the early church. We can easily romanticize it, but it must have been unnerving as well as thrilling. The book of Acts records an intense period of cultural and religious changes, a rollercoaster ride of new experiences, challenges, and learning at the leading of the Holy Spirit. The Spirit is sometimes alluded to in terms of chrism oil, for healing or blessing. In Acts, the allusion is not only to oil as blessing but also to engine oil—freeing things up, getting things moving! Before we look more closely at this story, let's frame it in a slightly broader context with our mission-shaped church lenses on.

In the earlier study on the Day of Pentecost, Acts was referred to as a book of ripples: from Jerusalem, to Judea and Samaria, to the ends of the earth, and outwards. Similarly, some suggest the book of Acts can be regarded as a series of waves of the missionary Spirit of God. The first wave is the Pentecost event—the mission to the Jews. The second wave is the persecution of the Jewish believers in Jerusalem causing them to flee the city (Acts 7). Without suggesting that God is directly responsible for the persecution or the death of Stephen, some point out that the believers aren't doing what God instructed. Like many Christian groups, they've gotten too settled and therefore need to be unsettled and propelled into mission as partners of the missionary Spirit. The third wave is this story of

Cornelius and Peter, which opens the Christian mission to non-Jews and is sometimes known as the Gentile Pentecost. Other waves are identified, but they don't concern us here. Whether ripples or waves, however, the notion of movement, outwards movement, geographically, culturally, and religiously is clear in the book of Acts.

> Pause . . .
>
> *To what extent do we regard unsettling things like grief, persecution, or a crisis as the impetus for engaging in more mission-mindedness, producing new aspects of faith and service?*

We note too that chapters 8, 9, and 10 of Acts consist of three conversion stories, and together these illustrate Jesus' command to his disciples that they are to be his witnesses, *in Jerusalem, Judea and Samaria, and to the ends of the earth.* Acts 8 tells of the conversion of an Ethiopian, an exotic Gentile African with some status, who not only receives the gospel but reaches out eagerly and grasps it with gratitude and joy. He represents those from the *ends of the earth.* Acts 9 tells of the conversion of Saul who becomes Paul, a Jew and a Pharisee. Saul is *the* enemy of followers of the Way of Christ, yet he becomes a believer. The gospel has power over its enemies, even those belonging to *Jerusalem.* Then in Acts 10, is the story of Cornelius, a Roman Godfearer (not Jewish by birth and therefore a Gentile) but nonetheless one who believes in the One True God of the Jews. Cornelius is regarded in much the same way as Samaritans: not completely beyond the pale but equally not fully or properly orthodox! The overall message? Those from *Jerusalem, Judea and Samaria and the ends of the earth*—in effect, everyone—can receive Christ through the witness of his followers empowered and enabled by the missionary Spirit of God.

> *Pause...*
>
> *Do you believe that everyone can receive Christ through the witness of his followers empowered and enabled by the missionary Spirit of God?*
>
> *What might prevent this from appearing not to be the case? And what might be done to rectify that?*

The Big Holy Spirit of Prevenient, Saving, and Sanctifying Grace

As advocates of mission-shaped church, reimagined evangelism, and fresh expressions, we talk about a "big" Holy Spirit—

- big, in the sense that the Spirit is more than was seen or declared by charismatic renewal, precious though those insights are,
- big, in that the Spirit of God in the Acts—and throughout the New Testament—is much more than the false conception of a tame pet of the early church,
- big, in that the missionary Spirit of God has a big mission, God's mission, in which the church of Christ is invited, required, and expected to play its part.

Those who study the Acts of the Apostles note that the Spirit of God is always going before. The believers and apostles are always playing catch-up. This is so in the story of Peter and Cornelius, and it's also a common experience of ordinary Christians today who engage in mission or evangelism.

We've outlined earlier the Wesleyan emphases on God's grace, and particularly about prevenient, saving, and sanctifying grace as aspects of that divine grace. In this story of Peter and Cornelius, we witness the saving and sanctifying activity of the Holy Spirit of God, but particularly prevenient grace at work.

Martyn Recalls:

When I was a tutor and professor at Cliff College, we'd send small teams of students to local churches who had invited them to share in mission in their neighborhoods. The team would gather in the College chapel for prayer just before setting off. "Why are you going to (whatever place) on this mission?" I'd ask them. An occasional response was this: "We're going to take Jesus to the poor people there." After the mission, when the team returned and we met again in the chapel for a debrief, I'd say, "So, you were going to take Jesus to the folk there—what happened?" Invariably came the reply, "Jesus was already there!" "So, what have you been doing these past two weeks then?" I'd ask, with a twinkle in my eye. "We saw what God was doing, and we joined in," they replied. Because even beginners in mission-shaped things quickly get to know something of the prevenient Spirit of God.

Pause...

Do we recognize the prevenient work of the Holy Spirit in all people and all circumstances in terms of our evangelism and mission?

What differences to our evangelistic and mission plans and activities might occur if we appreciated more fully the prevenient work of God in all people and places?

In this story, Cornelius is clearly someone in whom the Spirit of God is about her prevenient work. Cornelius is devout, plainly seeking God, and God goes to some lengths to be found. Peter too goes on a journey—both physically and spiritually. He's going to have to decide at various points whether to accept that God works in ways he hasn't considered possible or appropriate, and then choose how to respond.

We might wonder why God involved Peter in this story at all. Cornelius is praying, and God is clearly listening. Why didn't God just zap Cornelius there and then? Or why didn't God just send Cornelius to Joppa to meet Peter from the start? Why all this to-ing and fro-ing up and down from Caesarea to Joppa? Acts 10 could be half its length!

The answer is, of course, that both Cornelius and Peter need to be changed. Both learn that to spiritually grow entails leaving comfort zones and travelling to where others are. By the end of the story, both have different insights into God's will and ways than they had at the beginning. A repeated theme in Acts is made loud and clear. The salvation offered in Christ is for everyone. The mission of God will not be bounded or confounded by the restrictions and practices of ancient Judaism *or* believers in Christ that God calls to share the mission.

Pause...

Recall an occasion when you or your church left your comfort zone and went to where others are and talk together about it.

If you can't think of one—plan one.

The Mind-bending, Faith-changing Vision of Food

We find Simon Peter at the house of Simon the tanner. Simon the tanner was no doubt a Jew, but also a person whose occupation was considered by some Jews to be at the very least of dubious nature, if not unclean. Peter is going to make a journey to another unclean house, and it's while he's there at Simon's place, with the smells of animal hides in the air and unsavory tannin processes all around him, that Peter has the mind-bending, faith-changing vision of food.

We're told plainly that it's God who produces the vision rather than a satanic counterfeiter. The clue is the inclusion of Lord as Peter rejects the invitations to eat. It's the same clue Luke uses in Saul's conversion story a chapter earlier when he says to the risen Jesus, "Who are you, *Lord?*"

That's important, because the foodstuff lowered on the sheet includes food that is ritually both clean and unclean, the whole being defiled by being together. An immediate assumption of Jewish and Jewish-Christian hearers of this story would be that this vision didn't come from God, but Luke is making it clear that it did. Imagine the conversation:

"Rise Peter, kill and eat."

"No way. . . . Lord. It's against the Law—with a capital T—everybody knows that!"

"Yes Peter, I know the Law. I made it! Now rise, kill, and eat."

"You must be joking. . . . Lord? This is a test, isn't it? So, you'll be pleased I'm not falling for it . . ."

God, getting exasperated (does God get exasperated?), "Peter, I say what's clean and unclean, not you. Now rise and eat."

"But . . . Lord, I've never touched stuff like this in my life . . . and I'm not starting now."

And of course, he doesn't. The food is taken up into heaven, and we might wonder at what point Peter realizes that he's been involved in another threefold denial. He's in a real dilemma. Talk about a no-win situation. Whatever he does, he isn't sure he's doing what God wants or what he believes is right. Perhaps he says to himself, "Why am I so uptight? After all, I spent three years with the Lord Jesus who ate with sinners and wasn't exactly known for his fastidiousness about ritual cleanliness. And he wasn't exactly affirming about those who made that the be-all-and-end-all." We don't know. But we do know that when a group sent from Cornelius appears the next day and asks him to go with them to an unclean Gentile house in Caesarea, he goes.

Luke drops little pearls into the text for us. We're meant to note where Peter was—in Joppa. That's meant to jog the memories of readers about another figure staying in Joppa: Jonah. Jonah, like Peter, is asked to go to Gentiles and declare the gracious word of the Lord to them. Jonah, like Peter and many others, struggles with the concept of who's in and who's out of the reach of God's mercy and grace. Possibly Luke means us to recall Peter's original and full name too, because somewhat unusually he refers to it several times in this story—"Simon bar (that is, son of) Jonah." Here, however, the resonant similarities end. Jonah walks out of Joppa and heads as far away from the Gentiles to whom God commands him to go to as he can, and the rest of the book of Jonah is basically about what happens when you disobey God. Perhaps Simon bar Jonah might at one time have done the same. But Peter, an apostle of Jesus Christ, a sent one, a sent one who hasn't yet gone very far, with the mind-bending faith-changing vision of unclean food fresh in his mind, is about to make a momentous journey. He turns and heads towards Caesarea with a group of Gentiles.

Look at the world today. Look at your communities and declare that the lesson of the vision of food isn't as challenging and potentially trans-formative today as it was then. Is it any surprise that in small and different ways God is raising up new communities of faith that go rather than constantly invite people to come? That breaks the power of the rules of "We've always done it this way," and "We've always thought this way."

Clearly the God of mission reserves the right to act in new ways, ways that break with older rules, even rules God made. In fact, without such rule changing, there's no way that the mission to the "ends of the earth" can be fulfilled. It would be "from Jerusalem to . . . Jerusalem!" While Peter and other leading apostles believe in nationalistic, cultural, and reli-gion bound rules, there's no way an essentially closed Jewish faith of that time can become an open Christian faith, no way the death of Christ can be understood to be an act of grace, free, full, and for all, no way that most of us could ever have become Christians at all.

"Lord," we pray, "Renew our church. Give us a zeal for you and a heart for others. May we see people come to know you and love you. Use us in your purpose." It's a great prayer. God says, "I'd love to, but I have to break some rules to do so. . . ." There are times, and many believe we are now in such a time, when the leading of the Spirit supersedes our received ways of being disciples and being church and offers a new and bigger vision. In such times, however painful it is to stay with the old ways with, all their familiar appeal, is to be in the wrong place and slowly get left behind. We are left behind not only from those we know we are meant to love and serve but left behind by the prevenient Spirit of mission, which is always going ahead of us.

Pause...

What rules is it time to break in your church regarding the way it does things? Why?

Do you think you and your church need to go through a new conversion? If so, explore how that might come about.

If your church was to choose to go to a group of people they have never had anything to do with, what group of people would that be?

What religious rules do you think God might need to break today for the sake of God's mission?

Inside the Unclean, Blessed House

As the crow flies, it was about thirty miles from Joppa to Caesarea. Peter had travelled many longer trips, but not many as significant in terms of spreading the Christian faith. He arrives at the house of Cornelius and is invited in. Cornelius has no idea how to act but is deeply respectful. He falls at Peter's feet, and you can almost sense the embarrassment in Peter, not only in human terms, but also that he has become virtually an object of reverence! Cornelius may have produced food he thought Peter could eat. We don't know. Yet these finer points of hospitality or worship earn no rebuke from Peter, and we must read the text as a rather bemused, "Please get up. I'm only human like you are." For his part, Peter invites Cornelius to tell his story before Peter speaks. Then, in a spirit of affirmation—which is so easy to underestimate because we just can't fully understand how a Jew would feel being in the house of a Gentile at that time—Peter declares the gospel as it arises out of Cornelius' own story, and the Holy Spirit in pure delight falls upon and fills them all.

The sensitivity of this encounter deserves noting and offers some hints and clues in terms of our own role as witnesses to Jesus Christ today committed to appropriate, reimagined evangelism. Mutual respect. An invitation to share. Careful listening. Gracious responding.

Possibly it's because of centuries of having power and privilege, respectability, and influence that the Christian church is much more used to talking than listening, telling people what's what rather than inviting them to share, assuming it already knows rather than learning from others. Assumptions like these remain so deeply ingrained in our spiritual self-perceptions, our worship and liturgy, our body language and communications, that we haven't yet fully realized how little truth is left in them or what poor mission and evangelism they now are. So, though it doesn't feel it at the time, it's a good day when a local church realizes that all they have left to rely on is what Peter had—the ready help of the Spirit of God and the startling realization that the gospel really is Good news for everyone. Peter almost certainly had much the same internal struggle as local churches today. "I'm a member of the chosen race. I'm one of God's favorites. We keep the rules. We guard the gates. We're right!" But he comes to say, "God has shown me that I must not call anyone common or unclean, I now see God has no favorites." The world has changed—and for the better.

Many local churches today find themselves on much the same sort of journey as Peter. In another time of protracted turbulence and profound change, we too are being presented with challenging lessons by the Spirit of God who isn't content to live wholly inside the parameters of what we regard as normal or acceptable. Many things that have long been and still exist have passed their sell-by date. One common consequence of believing in God's prevenient grace is that we find it in people and places we think ought not to be! Christian communities and ways of being both Christians and church are created that others think can't be right. Like Peter, we must decide how to respond. Do we hunker down and retrench into what we know and like? As gatekeepers of resources and tradition, do we ensure that the rules make it virtually impossible for the *new* to flourish among us? Or do we change in order that we don't find ourselves parting company with what the missionary Spirit of God is doing? These are the very issues that churches seeking to be more profoundly mission-shaped face, tackle, and respond to with courage, openness, grace, and resolve.

Pause...

How will your church respond to these challenges about changing rules and stay in step with the Holy Spirit of mission and renewal?

Acts 10 is usually referred to as the conversion of Cornelius, but it is possibly even more significantly the continuing conversion of Peter. We have already written about Peter's conversion and call, but it is worth asking, just when was Peter converted? When he left his nets by the lakeside and first began to follow a young rabbi? Yes. After his denial when he confessed that he loved Jesus by the lakeside? Yes. When the Spirit fell on him at Pentecost, and he began to preach? Yes. Was he converted here, in a place and among people he's assumed all his life to be outside the scope of God love and salvation, until he realizes that God grace is for everyone, free full and for all? Yes. Yes, because conversion is a lifelong, continuing process of being shaped by God's grace, both for individuals *and for churches*. Yes, because conversion isn't so much about bringing God into our lives as bringing ourselves—individually and corporately—deeper into the life and purposes of God. Therefore, the communities of disciples we call local churches aren't ours to do with what we like. They're God's to do with whatever a God of mission might choose.

In this story, Luke makes clear that following a missionary God means crossing thresholds, transcending established rules, changing our minds, inviting strangers into our world, and allowing ourselves to enter theirs. We realize that in doing so, far from parting company with the Holy Spirit, we stay in step with her. Churches seeking to be more profoundly mission-shaped and committed to reimagined evangelism and fresh expressions need to learn such lessons and experience the pain and thrills of such conversions.

> Pause . . .
>
> "Mutual respect. An invitation to share. Careful listening. Gracious responding." To what extent is this the mood and tone of the witness and evangelism of your church?
>
> Are you able to say, about yourself and your church, "God has shown me that I must not call anyone common or unclean, I now see God has no favorites"?
>
> How is the continuing process of conversion and mission-mindedness going for you and your congregation?

Changed Lives! (Acts 16: 6–34)

To be used by the Holy Spirit of mission to enable new Christians to be made, and existing Christians to be deepened in their discipleship, is a critical test of being church as far as advocates of mission-shaped churches and fresh expressions are concerned. It wouldn't be overstating the case to say that the apparent inability of large numbers of inherited churches to make disciples of Christ today is a key reason for the need to create more fresh expressions and recommit to the pursuit of authentic and reimagined evangelism. But whether inherited or fresh, making disciples is vital. Disciple-making is the acid test of all churches.

While the great majority of local churches today are communities of people who are much the same as each other rather than significantly diverse and distinct, the book of Acts records an astounding ability to make authentic disciples of Jesus among people of very different cultures, classes, languages, and abilities. This passage in Acts 16 is one such and tells of three people changed by encountering believers in Christ. A good number of the reflections we offer here arise from hearing Chip Freed (a United Methodist pastor in Ohio talk about this passage in relation to his diverse, multiethnic congregation, and we readily and properly acknowledge that here. The Conferences Ken has led as Bishop are widely diverse, and Methodist Central Hall Westminster (the church in central London which Martyn led until relatively recently) has more than 30 different language and ethnic groupings in its membership. Sadly, such congregations are an all too rare species, but one laden with prophetic mission potency for today.

The life-changing stories are of Lydia, a rich business woman, an unnamed slave girl being trafficked as a fortune teller, and a jailor, and an ordinary working man. None of these stories are included in Acts accidentally or incidentally. That they come one after the other is not mere happenstance. Luke knows what he's doing. We should also note as we read this passage section by section that Luke is now himself a member of the missionary group. References to "they" did this and that (see Acts 16:6-7), change to "we" did this and that (see Acts 16:10-11), suggesting that Luke is offering an eye-witness account. Not surprisingly, these are often referred to as the "we" passages in Acts.

1. Lydia: Verses 6 to 13 set the scene, and verses 14 and 15 tell us about Lydia.

    They went through the region of Phrygia and Galatia, having been forbidden by the Holy Spirit to speak the word in Asia. When they had come opposite Mysia, they attempted to go into Bithynia, but the Spirit of Jesus did not allow them; so, passing by Mysia, they went down to Troas. During the night Paul had a vision: there stood a man of Macedonia pleading with him and saying, "Come over to Macedonia and help us." When he had seen the vision, we immediately tried to cross over to Macedonia, being convinced that God had called us to proclaim the good news to them. We set sail from Troas and took a straight course to Samothrace, the following day to Neapolis, and from there to Philippi, which is a leading city of the District of Macedonia and a Roman colony. We remained in this city for some days. On the sabbath day we went outside the gate by the river, where we supposed there was a place of prayer; and we sat down and spoke to the women who had gathered there. A certain woman named Lydia, a worshipper of God, was listening to us; she was from the city of Thyatira and a dealer in purple cloth. The Lord opened her heart to listen eagerly to what was said by Paul. When she and her household were baptized, she urged us, saying, "If you have judged me to be faithful to the Lord, come and stay at my home." And she prevailed upon us.

Lydia is a businesswoman, a trader in purple cloth, which was highly expensive owing to the rarity of the dye used, which came from crushing thousands of a certain kind of seashell. The shell in question was found almost exclusively in the coastal area around Thyatira, in modern Turkey, from where Lydia originated. She's a foreigner, an immigrant, a woman who may well be a widow, or her husband is away. We can assume she's wealthy. She certainly has a house and household able to accommodate the missionary party. She's described as *a worshipper of God,* probably suggesting that she professed belief in the One True God of the Jews but wasn't a full convert to Judaism—like Cornelius.

On the Sabbath, Paul and the others go to where they expect to find *a place of prayer,* and since they go outside the city walls, we can assume that they sought an act of Jewish worship. However, instead of a synagogue, they come across a group of women meeting for prayer. Some say that this suggests that there wasn't the required number of Jewish males (ten) to formally create a synagogue in Philippi, making clear its dominant paganism. No doubt introductions were made, and the women invite Paul to speak. We don't have the text of his sermon, but we do know that Lydia—and others—responded to it. The text says, *the Lord opened her heart* to what was said, which is a way of saying that she got it. Then Lydia invites them to her house. She and her household are baptized, and her home becomes the first Christian church in Philippi (Acts 16:40).

Notably, the first thing this new Christian does is open her home. Where God opens the heart, God opens the home. It's people who have been accepted who most often become accepting. It's those who come to realize that they're invited into a relationship with God who most often live lives shaped by that invitation. If anything, the text hints that it's Paul and his group who are reluctant to agree to enter her home rather than Lydia being reluctant to invite them. She insists in providing hospitality. As with Peter in Acts 10, there's the suggestion that going into a female Gentile's home remains a challenge.

Both offering invitation and hospitality *and* being open to receive it is mission potent today and is a common factor in very many fresh expressions of church. It's no surprise that in his book, *The Five Practices of Fruitful Congregations,* Robert Schnase lists radical hospitality first. Open doors. Inviting spaces. Non-judgmental environments. Places of sanctuary, blessing, and challenge. These are the signs that a gracious God has moved in. How evident is all this in our homes and leisure spaces, congregations, and churches? All churches can be invitational, but mission-shaped and fresh expressions advocates emphasize the value and need of being where others are. Our churches are used to inviting people to come, but less used to going to someone else's space and place and receiving as readily as giving. Our churches almost naturally think of themselves as host and much less often as guest. They usually assume that they will be in charge and call the shots. Yet, it is the servant nature of the Christian church that is much needed today. As John Robinson put it long ago, "the first characteristic of a servant is that he (sic) lives in someone else's house, not his own." To be among others, standing alongside each other, in mutual partnership not dependency, humbly bearing witness to Christ, is to form mission-potent church environments today.

Paul had intended to go east, interestingly into the very region Lydia came from. The Spirit said no through a vision of a Macedonian man saying, *come over and help us.* As a result, Paul changes plans and goes west. So, the "going before" Spirit of God brings Lydia from western Turkey, east to Philippi. Then the Spirit tells Paul who wanted to go to western Turkey to go west instead, and he comes to Philippi. The Spirit brings them together. Lydia becomes a Christian believer, and Paul is given opportunity to rethink his attitudes about hospitality and possibly about women! If you'd asked Paul on the journey to Philippi if his aim was to start a church of believers with a group of women, he'd have probably laughed and said, "no way." We can only wonder at what point he realized that his Macedonian man turned out to be an Asian woman!

Pause . . .

In what ways does your church both offer invitation and hospitality and demonstrate an openness to receive it?

Does your church tend to regard itself as host? In what ways might it deliberately seek to be a guest? How, and with whom?

2. The slave girl: Acts 16: 16 -19 tells the story of an un-named slave girl, a fortune teller with an evil spirit.

    One day, as we were going to the place of prayer, we met a slave-girl who had a spirit of divination and brought her owners a great deal of money by fortune-telling. While she followed Paul and us, she would cry out, "These men are slaves of the Most High God, who proclaim to you a way of salvation." She kept doing this for many days. But Paul, very much annoyed, turned and said to the spirit, "I order you in the name of Jesus Christ to come out of her." And it came out that very hour. But when her owners saw that their hope of making money was gone, they seized Paul and Silas and dragged them into the marketplace before the authorities.

The New Testament Greek text describes her having a python spirit, as in a snake, probably referring to the ornate snake sculpture that guarded the Delphic Oracle in central Greece. The Greek god Apollo was said to have killed the actual snake and its ability to predict the future, then entered the high priestess and spread through her to other women. Possessing a python spirit, or being possessed by a python spirit (probably both) meant that the girl could foretell the future. This ability was exploited by her owners to make them rich. She was effectively being trafficked.

Paul and his companions may be going to the place of prayer, probably with Lydia and others now in the group, when they first meet the unnamed girl. She then follows them about, probably for many days, exclaiming to all and sundry, "these men are servants of the most-high God and proclaiming the way of salvation." This is true of course, though whether she was being sarcastic or declaring it as discerned truth, we're not sure. We also don't know if her words assisted or hampered the groups evangelistic witness. But we do know that Paul gets sick and tired of it. The words used in the original Greek text suggest a mixture of emotions. Paul is *aggravated* and *angry* by her shouting but comes increasingly to *grieve* about the exploitative and abusive situation in which the girl finds herself. He is also *saddened* by her double bondage, being bound to both an evil spirit and evil traffickers. This complicated combination of emotions means that Paul doesn't tell her to leave them alone but commands that the evil spirit come out of her, and the name of Jesus sets her free from both types of bondage.

This mixture of emotions and reactions is common to churches seeking to be mission-shaped. Irritation and anger at people tend to give way to anger at what has happened to them. Such church communities become grief stricken and saddened in such a way that they get involved in engaging and seeking to ameliorate the situation. They seek to become agents of healing and transformative grace. That is one reason why a sizeable proportion of fresh expressions of church take root in or emerge from communities of broken and needy people.

We don't know for certain whether the girl is converted and joins the church at Lydia's place. But the fact that her story is sandwiched between two others of people who clearly become believers suggests she was, and she did. Though it likely took some time, because we're witnessing someone who enters the fellowship with considerable baggage and history and who has some way to travel before they can accept God's love and saving grace. Perhaps at first, all the girl knows is that her life has been changed and this group of people have something to do with it. Only slowly, two steps forward, one back, does she draw a little closer to them and to Christ.

The slave girl reminds us of some people we've encountered as pastors, the young man who started attending a young adult congregation, for example. He had no church background, a dodgy past, no biblical literacy, no Christian language, nothing except a readiness to say yes to Christ which was, as it always is in every instance, the beginning of the story of his new life, not its end. An initial conversion owed much more to the accepting friendship offered by the congregation than any deep, cognitive understanding of repentance, forgiveness, atonement, or salvation. His first contribution to the shared prayers was unforgettable. "Lord . . . thank you for these guys and for bringing me here. It's f*****g brilliant!" There was a long pause then the group responded enthusiastically, "Amen"!

Or the young woman with many issues, a member of a youth fellowship in a past church assignment. Some conditions were obvious— she was anorexic—and others only became observed or disclosed over weeks and months: about rejection, betrayal, abuse, and mental fragility. These complicated, multiple conditions were being properly addressed by various professionals and treatments, but also by members in the local church, who offered compassionate gifts of patience, time, support, healing prayer, gentle ministry, friendship, love, and acceptance. The woman will never fit the stereotype of the articulate or stable Christian, yet her ability to share her growing yet fragile faith and befriend other people who have walked paths similar to hers is amazing.

Now, of course, every local church can tell stories like that, surely. Well, many can, but increasingly and sadly, many can't or can't any longer. They have become churches that receive or engage few new people. Most times it wasn't their intention to become like this, and they're saddened or even depressed at the fact. What is sadder and more depressing still, however, are the many local churches that are simply not bothered. They are content as they are, and by action if not rhetoric, clearly regard ministry and appropriate evangelism among others as neither their problem nor their mission. Large numbers of local churches have become, either intentionally or unconsciously, somewhat monochrome communities, populated by people who at one level appear different, but at another, in very telling ways, are very much alike. In consequence, all the activities in the church—the mood, and style of worship, the causes to which they donate, the events which they organize, and the voluntary help they offer—fit what *they* like. Which is fine—except for everyone else who's different!

> *Pause...*
>
> What would be the mixture of emotions in your congregation if the slave girl, the young man, or young woman described above lived in your neighborhood and started coming along to church?
>
> Would such people be turned away or receive ministry, do you think?

Advocates of mission-shaped churches talk more than most about the barriers and obstacles that often exist in congregations. They do so, because they believe almost all such barriers are mission debilitating rather than mission enabling. They put people off. Preventing people with opportunities to experience God is a serious business. To identify barriers of local church folk (ones they are genuinely unaware of) then address and remove them is mission critical work. We tend to talk about the body language of a local church. A church's body language isn't so much what it says but what it signals and indicates. "We're very friendly," we say, and we believe it. But the reality is that only those who fit in found us to be so. Those who didn't are no longer around to comment. "We welcome everyone," we say, and we believe it. But there's a marked homogeneity about our communities. Those who were different came and went quickly or never arrived at all. Some decided, often unknown to us, that they needed to be richer, better educated, better dressed, or just better to join us. The story we like to tell about ourselves isn't necessarily the way we're experienced by others.

Perfectionism is a particularly damaging type of church body language. Despite our sincere belief that we all fall short of the glory of God, our body language sometimes declares that we're a community that has got it all together. We signal that we're not the community of the broken but the whole, not the sinful but the saved, with the consequence that those whose lives are shaped by brokenness, addiction, grief, abuse, or repeated human failure quickly sense they have no place among us. All one happy family here. Don't spoil it. Sinners need not apply. Ironic, isn't it, that of all things, this is how we articulate our spiritual aspirations, our desire to be better Christians, that sometimes separates us from those whom the missionary Spirit of God places within our midst? Tragic, isn't it, when we become faith families where there's no place for the slave girl? She's just too broken, too needy, too different, too heavy duty, too slow to change to likely ever be able to become one of us.

Pause...

How would you describe the body language of your church?

What is the story we tell about ourselves? How do we tell our stories in ways that assume a desired perfectionism? Do you think your church suffers from perfectionism at all?

Of course, fresh expressions of church are just as susceptible to all this, as inherited churches, and both can be mission-shaped to a larger or lesser degree. But it's the apparent inability or unwillingness of many inherited churches to meaningfully meet and befriend the increasing numbers of different people who live among and around them. That's a key reason why fresh expressions are so needed. A crucial part of their freshness is an intention to live and form church among so-called unchurched and de-churched people. They actively seek to be church together with those who not only have no church, but often have no knowledge or perceived need of church. We reach new places and new people in new ways, as the Fresh Expressions movement in the United Kingdom often puts it.

Such churches are propelled into the Spirit-led messiness and costliness of being communities of the very different, contributing not only service but sharing influence, offering not only ministry but sharing leadership, giving not only time but sharing ownership. There are no blueprints, no guarantees, and many failures. But whenever a church community, whether it self-identifies as fresh, inherited, or anything else, becomes a faith family in which a once possessed and abused slave girl might find love and acceptance, in which, very slowly, she might experience new and real life, then the Spirit of the Living God rejoices.

We don't know definitively if the slave girl made it. But if so, what a great church at Lydia's place it was!

3.   The Jailer: The story of the jailer is found in Acts 16:23-34. The owners of the slave girl seize Paul and Silas and bring them before the magistrates who order them to be stripped and beaten.

After they had been severely flogged, they were thrown into prison, and the jailer was commanded to guard them carefully. When he received these orders, he put them in the inner cell and fastened their feet in the stocks.

About midnight Paul and Silas were praying and singing hymns to God, and the other prisoners were listening to them. Suddenly there was such a violent earthquake that the foundations of the prison were shaken. At once all the prison doors flew open, and everyone's chains came loose. The jailer woke up, and when he saw the prison doors open, he drew his sword and was about to kill himself because he thought the prisoners had escaped. But Paul shouted, "Don't harm yourself! We are all here!"

The jailer called for lights, rushed in and fell trembling before Paul and Silas. He then brought them out and asked, "Sirs, what must I do to be saved?"

They replied, "Believe in the Lord Jesus, and you will be saved—you and your household." Then they spoke the word of the Lord to him and to all the others in his house. At that hour of the night the jailer took them and washed their wounds; then immediately he and all his household were baptized. The jailer brought them into his house and set a meal before them; he was filled with joy because he had come to believe in God—he and his whole household.

The jailor was possibly ex-Roman military, a hard man who could take prisoners with their backs raw and bleeding, throw them into prison, fasten their feet, lock the door, and go sleep soundly. While at midnight, in blackness, in prison, in pain, and in shackles, Paul and Silas are singing praises to God and declaring their faith in Christ. Lord, how we need to learn to not let our circumstances determine our faith and witness!

Pause . . .

To what extent does your church let circumstances determine faith and witness?

Then there's the earthquake which rocks the building and opens every cell. The jailer has no doubt heard them singing. It's possible that he's heard what happened to the slave girl and her exclamations that Paul and Silas are men of God. But whether he did or not, the earth moving is the clincher. Assuming where the blame will land, the jailer is about to fall on his sword when Paul calls to him with the result that he cries out to them to be saved. So, Paul and Silas lead him to Christ—a man who in the hours previous will likely have cursed them, spit on them, abused them, beaten them, and treated them as less than nothing. Lord, make us more forgiving and gracious!

Luke notes that the first thing the newly saved jailer does is wash the wounds of Paul and Silas (another example of hospitality). Then he and his family are baptized, as Lydia's household were. A lovely but probably romantic thought is that Paul may have baptized them in the common bowl used to tend his wounds? In any event, the jailer washed them, and then was washed, and Luke tells how these Jewish Christian leaders and this Gentile pagan family joyfully share a meal together. As with the slave girl, we're not told whether the jailer and his family join the church at Lydia's home, though the reference to "brothers and sisters" in Acts 16:40 suggests a growing community of faith which would likely include this newly converted family.

Have you heard the one about the rich woman, the slave girl, and the jailer? It sounds like the opening line of a joke, but the insights offered are mission critical, so to ignore them is no laughing matter. We're meant to note the stark *differences* in the stories of three people becoming believers in Christ.

- They're *racially* different. Lydia is an Asian migrant in Greco-Roman cosmopolitan Philippi. The slave girl is regarded as a non-person, and the jailer is almost certainly a Roman citizen.
- They're *economically* different. Lydia is rich and respectable. The slave girl owns nothing, and the jailer is an ordinary working family man. What do you imagine their respective upbringings were like?
- The *circumstances* in which they encounter Christ are different. Lydia was at a prayer meeting; the slave girl was on the streets; and the jailer was doing his job.
- They're *psychologically* different. Lydia is a *cognitive* type, wanting the gospel explained to her. The slave girl is *experiential*. She needs an encounter with God that's stronger than the forces that bind her. The jailer too witnesses what he regards as a powerful work of God but is clearly a *practical* man. He follows orders, and he's got routines. He responds to what happens in logical and sensible ways: my prisoners have all escaped, I must pay the price for failure. I am wrong about these men. I will act differently towards them.
- They're at different points in a *spiritual journey*. Lydia is clearly seeking God; the slave girl is clearly serving evil; and the jailer is clearly unshaped by any notion of religion other than doing his

duty to the Roman pantheon of gods—until he comes across Paul and Silas.

And yet, they each respond to the same gospel proclaimed by word *and* action by the mission band led by Paul and are received into the same community of Christ. As Luke constantly reminds us in the Acts, God's grace in Jesus Christ is for everyone.

Wouldn't you just love to be a fly on the wall of the church in Philippi meeting at Lydia's house? What a holy mess it probably was! Lost people act lost for a long time after they're first found. Broken people act broken a long time after they begin to be made whole. Inbred culture and manners and norms persist long after the Holy Spirit mediates Christ's saving grace. But here's the marvelous thing. Church for everybody can change anybody. At its essence, that's what this passage in Acts is about. The gospel of Jesus—and the church of Jesus that arises from it—is the most potent entity in the world to bring people together. Lord, forgive us when so often we are not!

Pause...

How like the church at Lydia's home is your local church?

In what ways would you like your congregation to become more like that community in Philippi?

In Paul's many letters to fledgling Christian churches, he's not always warm and cuddly. Some local churches get a real bee in their ear. Many years after these events in Philippi first took place, Paul writes to the Philippians, "I thank my God every time I remember you. . . . I always pray with joy because of your partnership in the gospel from the first day until now, being confident of this, that he who began a good work in you will carry it on to completion until the day of Christ Jesus" (Philippians 1:3-6). He writes to a healthy church without deep criticism.

In the previous study, we suggested that Peter as much as Cornelius was converted in the sense that he continued to have to respond to new things God was teaching him. That's also true of Paul here. Paul a Jew, a strict Jew, who like millions of Jews then (and some even now) prayed this kind of prayer each day "I thank you Lord that you have not made me a Gentile, that you have not made me a woman, and that you have not made me a slave." At the clear leading of the Holy Spirit, in pagan Philippi, a healthy church is started with a wealthy woman, a redeemed slave, and a Gentile working man! Alleluia!

Pause...

What do you think God is saying to you and your church through this study in Acts 16?

If you were to start a church plant or fresh expression in response to this study, where would it be, and among whom?

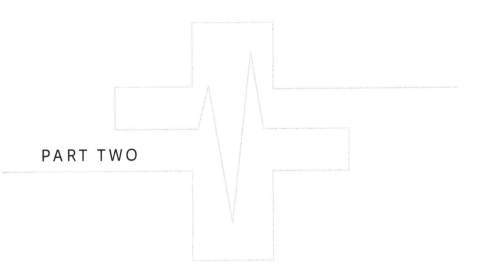

PART TWO

The Mission-shaped Church

Some Autobiographical History and Context

(For those who like to know a little about who's writing the book they're reading and why they've written it!)

Ken—A Testimony from the United States

I came to faith in Jesus Christ as a college student, through participation in a campus ministry group and while reading through the New Testament one spring. At some point along the way, this had become my story, a better one than I had been living, a better present and future than the one I had plotted out for myself. And so, I met with my pastor and was baptized as I made a profession of faith. Later that year, a small, inner-city church contacted me with an invitation to work with their youth. There were about twenty of them, alongside a worshiping congregation of seventy members over seventy years of age. I met with them for a couple of years. Again we read through the New Testament, and to be honest I was only a step ahead of them each week. We met Friday evenings, Sunday mornings, and Sunday evenings. Along the way, it dawned on all of them and me that they had never been baptized but had a desire to be baptized and become part of the Church. Again I met with my supervising pastor, and we set the date. On that Sunday, almost all of them walked down the aisle and presented themselves for baptism, made promises to God and to those present, and received the sacrament of Holy Communion.

These two experiences changed the trajectory of my life. Everything else has flowed from them. Had I missed them, I can only imagine the path I might have taken. I cannot imagine it being as abundant or as surprising as the journey I have been on, and indeed, the way is still unfolding.

Leading the youth group gave me a new sense of calling, which led to Divinity School. I had an education grounded in what I would call a generous orthodoxy—not fundamentalism—but a conviction that the scriptures and the Church could offer hope and possibility for all (of us) in need of salvation, grace, healing and amendment of life. My teachers at Duke led us deeply into the biblical texts, the great tradition, and the implications of all of this for ministry. In particular, several professors guided me toward an emerging appreciation for the Wesleyan order of salvation: image of God, prevenient grace, repentance, justification by faith, and sanctification.

I began to frame my earlier experiences in light of this knowledge. I came to realize that my decisions and acceptances were actually not a beginning but were situated in a family lineage—and in fact, my great-grandfather (a congregational pastor) had baptized me as an infant! I began to see God's prevenient grace there in my mother, who gave birth to me two months following her graduation from high school, in my grandparents and in teachers, coaches, and youth directors.

I took this new appreciation for the wideness of God's mercy into my first assignment, a four-church circuit in a very rural county in the foothills of the North Carolina Piedmont. One of the members, Bobby, would introduce me to every unchurched person in the community. He was, in fact, the evangelism class I never had in Divinity School. My predecessor in the circuit had become a traveling evangelist, and the churches were formed in his style and theology. For some time, I tried to mimic this, in order to gain their acceptance. At some point, I realized that I simply needed to find my own voice, and trust that God will give them and me what we all needed in this process. I became much happier, and I believe they were as well!

In the coming years, I would share my faith through teaching Bible studies, leading *Walk to Emmaus* and *Cursillo* retreats, preaching in camp meetings, and teaching evangelism in the Course of Study for Ministry at Duke. I began to integrate my practice with theory. I was influenced by Mortimer Arias' *Evangelization and the Kingdom of God*. In fact, Arias actually met with our students on one occasion. I went through the training in Basic Christianity with Billy Abraham and used his book, *The Logic of Evangelism*, for a decade with students.

During this time, I helped to plant a new church, and years later would be assigned to two large regional churches. The complexity of these churches and the experience with *Emmaus* and +retreats led me to the conviction that I had been too individualistic in my understanding of both the faith and the Church's mission. I went more deeply into learning about spiritual gifts, my own and those of others, and wrote a book entitled *The Gifted Pastor*. I could look back to see that Bobby, the lay leader in my first parish, had the gift of evangelism, a gift that I needed.

Through the grace of God these churches grew in membership and in professions of faith. Over time, I sensed a call to be open to the possibility of serving as a bishop, one that I knew within and one echoed by others. I served for a brief time in the mountains of Western North Carolina as a District superintendent, and there I saw the first fresh expression of church in my own experience—a small, traditional mountain parish that had birthed a weekly gathering for worship alongside a large outdoor center that featured rafting and water activities. It became the *River of Life* and attracted those whom the Church had difficulty reaching. With a colleague superintendent, we developed a network of experiments in faith-sharing across a fifteen-county region. This was deeply rewarding. We were reaching new people, and we were using a full complement of gifts.

I was elected a bishop of the United Methodist Church and assigned to Florida, a large, multi-ethnic and mostly urban Conference. I arrived having planted a new church but was increasingly convinced that fresh expressions of church like the *River of Life* was needed more than expensive property and salary-driven projects. I continued to learn from people like Graham Cray, Martyn Atkins, Angela Shier-Jones, and Rowan Williams about the United Kingdom experience. A leadership team was appointed, and the Fresh Expressions movement began among Florida Methodists. I am deeply grateful to Michael Beck and Audrey Warren, who have been at the heart of that work, among many others.

I found myself connecting the impulse toward a generous orthodoxy for the LGBTQIA community. For me, the good news of the gospel (which is grace) leads us in a lifelong journey toward holiness
(which is love of God and neighbor). This would become the basis for
another book: *Embracing the Wideness of God's Mercy*.

This move was less ideological than it was simply the evangelism
that was needed in our time and season. This would become central
to my work as president of our Global Council of Bishops. It would
be there that I sought to mediate between progressives (who often
did not understand my traditional theology) and conservatives (who
often did not appreciate my desire for inclusion).

All of this is the mystery of how the God who began a good work
in me will be faithful to complete it! I have not packaged this story
into a neat system. It is simply all grace. I have a deep desire that all
may know this grace and set out on their own journeys!

Martyn—A Testimony from Britain

2004 seemed ages ago or just the blink of an eye, depending on how
you look at it. But that was the year the book *Mission-Shaped Church*
was first published, and the *Fresh Expressions* initiative began in the
United Kingdom. By that time, I'd been an ordained presbyter (Elder)
in the British Methodist Church for over twenty years, having come
to faith in Christ at age seventeen, spent four years training in Manchester, and was in my fourth ministerial assignment. I recount my
first of multiple moments of conversion to mission-shaped church in
my book *Resourcing Renewal*.

> I can remember exactly when and where I was converted to
> the idea that the church is essentially missionary in nature
> and purpose. It was my first church appointment as a min-
> ister, and I had encouraged my devout largely aged congre-
> gation to have a 'lay witness weekend'. Essentially a review
> of local church life with a focus on renewal, it involved the
> visit of a number of (lay) Christians from around the country
> who led discussions, prayer and worship. It was Saturday

morning, and I joined a discussion group meeting on the disused stage in the church schoolroom on the agreed basis that, given it was a lay witness weekend, I didn't say anything. "What's the purpose of our church, why are we here?" asked the leader. "To invite people to join us," it was readily agreed.

"Yes, but why?" persisted the leader.

"Well," said one of my stewards earnestly, "we're all getting older and someone's got to do all the jobs—we can't go on forever."

It was as the whole group nodded their ready assent, and I bit my tongue, that I was converted to mission-shaped church thinking.[5]

For many, mission-shaped church thinking and talk of the need for fresh ways of being church started long before 2004. My increasing interest in such things resulted in me going to serve at Cliff College (a British Methodist training institution) in 1996 to teach evangelism, mission, and church renewal. My graduate students and I reveled in a large supply of resources. *Transforming Mission* by South African David Bosch was a key book.[6] He divided Christian history into several eras. He called them paradigms and treated his readers to a complex but magnificent overview of the theologies, practices, and meanings of Christian mission. Another must read was almost anything Lesslie Newbigin wrote after his retirement. *The Gospel in a Pluralist Society* for example, explored how Christian faith might best engage with a western society shaped by religious pluralism and ethnic diversity.[7] Newbigin suggested—very importantly in relation to our foci in

[5] Martyn Atkins, *Resourcing Renewal: Shaping Churches for the Emerging Future* (London: Epworth Press, 2010).

[6] David Bosch, *Transforming Mission: Paradigm Shifts in Theology of Mission* (New York: Orbis Books, 2011).

[7] Lesslie Newbglin, *The Gospel in a Pluralist Society* (Grand Rapids: Eerdmans Publishing, 1989)

this book—that the primary agency for making a Christian impact on public life (and thereby people found both inside and outside the church) is a congregation of women and men who believe the gospel and live by it. Then there were significant Papal Encyclicals like *Redemptoris Missio* that affirmed the Church's essential missionary nature and role as a means of meeting the needs of the contemporary world.[8]

It seemed that new books on mission-related subjects were published every month, each recognizing with varying degrees of seriousness the decline of the Church in the West and suggesting various responses and remedies. New Zealander Mike Riddell foretold the imminent collapse of institutional Church in *Threshold of the Future*,[9] while American Rick Warren wrote more optimistically in *The Purpose-Driven Church*.[10] Martin Robinson described *The Faith of the Unbeliever*, an increasingly common species of contemporary person who disowns traditional Christian beliefs and structure yet is not a believer in nothing at all.[11] Reflecting on the Billy Graham Mission England rallies in *To Reach a Nation*, Gavin Reid suggested that never again would Britain be effectively evangelized by crusades.[12] In *The Logic of Evangelism*, Billy Abraham asserted that almost all recent and contemporary evangelism was a reduced, poor version of what it was meant to be, which was in fact rich and full initiation

[8] John Paul II, *On the Permanent Validity of the Church's Missionary Mandate* (United States Catholic Conference, 1990).

[9] Mike Riddell, *Threshold of the Future: Reforming the Church in the Post-Christian West* (Society for Promoting Christia, 1998).

[10] Rick Warren, *The Purpose Driven Church: Growth Without Compromising Your Message* (Toronto: Harper Collins Canada, 1995).

[11] Martin Robinson, *The Faith of the Unbeliever: Building Innovative Relations* (Derby, CT: Monarch Books, 1994).

[12] Gavin Reid, *To Reach a Nation: The Challenge of Evangelism in a Mass-Media Age* (London: Hodder & Stoughton, 1987).

into the Kingdom of God.[13] And Australians Al Hirsch and Mike Frost offered an alternative, challenging future in *The Shaping of Things to Come—Innovation and Mission for the 21st Century Church.*[14] All these and many more were in the ether and known to those who wrote *Mission-Shaped Church.* What was different about that book wasn't its innovation, but that key mission themes were set out clearly and urged for adoption in an official report by a mainline historic denomination—the Church of England.

The *Fresh Expressions* initiative, also beginning in 2004, did not arrive out of nothing. Various types of cell church, house church, and church plants—to name but three species—were already well established. The 1990s was designated *A Decade of Evangelism* by the Church of England—an idea quickly adopted by several other United Kingdom denominations, including Methodism. It was in part a clear recognition of the serious decline of those denominations. One major initiative created for the decade by the Church of England was *Springboard,* a somewhat traditional engagement in evangelism led by well-known, excellent speakers going from place-to-place, preaching and inviting people to follow Christ.

By the early twenty-first century, both the *Decade of Evangelism* and *Springboard* had ended, and it was widely agreed that (often expensive and time hungry) evangelistic campaigns now achieved less than what was formerly assumed or hoped for. New, better ways of sharing and proclaiming Christian faith were very much needed. In late 2002, Rowan Williams became Archbishop of Canterbury, and his enthusiasm for such things was largely unknown. Positive signs were soon evident, however. Williams not only expanded the working party that would produce *Mission-Shaped Church,* but also heeded key learning reinforced by the *Decade* that effective and apt evangelism

---

[13] Billy Abraham, *The Logic of Evangelism* (Grand Rapids: Wm. B. Erdmans Publishing, 1989),

[14] Al Hirsch and Mike Frost, *The Shaping of Things to Come: Innovation and Mission for the 21st Century Church* (Grand Rapids: Baker Books, 2003).

was best rooted in the life, witness, and ministries of local churches. What was now needed wasn't *Springboard #2,* or a wholesale out-sourcing of evangelism to gifted evangelists, or a faint-hearted moratorium of all evangelistic ventures. Rather it was a well-resourced agency, encouraging and resourcing new ways of being church. In 2004, *Fresh Expressions (Ltd)* was born. Fittingly, given that the Church of England and the Methodist Church of Great Britain had entered a Covenant in November 2003, Fresh Expressions was from the beginning an ecumenical initiative of these two Churches (and in subsequent years several others).

Though it wasn't fully recognized or appreciated at the time, the *Mission-Shaped Church* book and the *Fresh Expressions* initiative were the inter-related, mutually enhancing textual and embodied resources of new emphases and understandings of mission, evangelism, and church by some of the historic mainline denominations in the United Kingdom.

Since 2004 and right down to today, an avalanche of materials, programs, books, blogs, vlogs, seminars, webinars, podcasts, in-person and online events and gatherings, initiatives, and experiments have come about, not to mention thousands of new ecclesial communities and pioneering ministries. We have seen no sign yet of learning, commitment, and innovation waning, either in the United Kingdom or, increasingly in recent years, around the world, and not least in the United States. Marvelous!

Ken and Martyn

Note, please, the use of marvelous. We are both deeply encouraging and supportive of mission-shaped church and fresh expressions, by which we mean not merely the book and initiative arriving in 2004, but the whole evolving movement. Virtually every insight, every project, every ministry, every experiment, every yearning, and every learning is encouraging to us, not because all fresh expressions are good and right and everything else is wrong. Some new initiatives are hopeless! Additionally, this is also not because we think more mission-shaped churches will, of themselves, reverse the steep decline and accelerating cultural marginalization of our own Methodist Churches, because we don't. The future doesn't lay in vain attempts to *return* to any version of a partly mythical successful past. We are not writing this because we're sick and tired of inherited church and have given up on it, because we're not and we haven't, as some of our previous books, like *Resourcing Renewal: Shaping Churches for the Emerging Future* and *Fresh Expressions: A New Kind of Methodist Church for People Not in Church* make clear.

If not these reasons, why then? Quite simply, we believe that the impulse urging mission-shaped churches, fresh expressions, and reimagined evangelism is of God. This can be put in terms of a divinely sent disquiet that things in church aren't as God wants them to be, or in more upbeat terms, that God wants to change and transform us all. We believe this movement is of God. We also believe it's not lacking God's guidance or anointing. This doesn't mean nothing can go wrong, that success is guaranteed, or that the anointing can't be frittered away, rejected, or abused. But it does mean that even in the most apparently stagnant and moribund of church congregations, the faltering first signs of openness and obedience to the God of mission cause God to smile. Yet, like all kinds of discipleship, the way ahead isn't easy or without cost.

For both of us—at least in terms of human agents of divine grace—everything flows from evangelism. Through the lives, lips, and Christian love of significant but perfectly ordinary people used of God, we both came to accept the gift of God's grace through faith in Jesus Christ. This has unfolded over the years in our sense of call to urge the Church to realize and embrace God's mission as its own mission, to be a sign of God's Kingdom, present with us in Jesus Christ, crucified and risen, and manifested in the enabling gifts of the Holy Spirit. God's gifts of grace can never be the exclusive possession of an individual or a group but are for everyone. So, although our own experiences of divine grace have been in the Wesleyan and Methodist stream of the Church, we hope those who are part of the precious One Body of Christ beyond our own tradition can and will readily join the conversation contained in these pages. All are welcome! Indeed, like our father in God John Wesley, we draw strength and hope from the great tradition. The Moravian Daily Texts, the Book of Common Prayer, and spiritual classics such as *The Imitation of Christ* are treasured, used resources for us both. These and others help provide a broad grounding for a mission-shaped evangelism which is an expression of the rich diversity of gifts belonging to the One Church of Jesus Christ.

Our Methodist tradition of Christian faith, like all others, possesses certain emphases, moods, tones, and even peculiarities! They're not better than those of other Christian traditions, nor are they unique, but they are particularly precious to Methodist disciples of Christ. Whether mere romanticism or not, such doctrinal emphases and patterns of discipleship are believed to have been given—or perhaps entrusted—to Methodism by God for the enrichment and benefit of the whole Church and the whole world. This can sound grand and lofty, but in fact offers no grounds for pride. Instead, it requires of Methodism a deep, continuing sense of commitment and responsibility to be the kind of churches and people God raised us up to be: obedient servants of The Servant Christ.

Several of these cherished and challenging Methodist themes lie at the heart of this book. All of them are found in the faith and work of John and Charles Wesley and indeed of scholars and practitioners right down to today, some of whom we are privileged to call our friends. First, we remain committed to rediscovering the essence of the earliest Church (primitive Christianity) and helping it to become alive and formed in the present time. Second, we continue to believe that offering Christ is at the heart of authentic Methodism. Consequently, that cannot be abandoned without a profound loss of identity and purpose. Hence, we make a case for gentle, gracious but nonetheless real evangelism, and urge participation in God's rich, deep mission: evangelism and mission which is diverse, intelligent, contextual, sensitive, and appropriate. Third, we recognize the need for fertile ways of enabling people today to become not simply *converts*—though we believe in conversion—but, crucially contemporary *disciples* of Christ, disciples outpoured in Christ's name, characterized by love, motivated by justice, mercy and peace, and committed to the transformation of the world and the health of the planet for the benefit of all. Fourth, we are convinced that the best environment in which all this can take place is in and through Christian communities and congregations. But—and it is a very significant but—in order to become what is intended by God that we become, we must practice radical openness and obedience to God and to the world and its wonder, wounds, needs, and peoples, all of which almost always dramatically reshapes the very life and being of local Christian communities. Our contending for better, reimagined evangelism, mission-shaped churches, and fresh expressions must be understood in this way: as potent vehicles given over to the leading of the missionary Holy Spirit of God.

Today, nearer the end of our active ministries than their beginnings, our passion for and commitment to exploring fresh ways of being church, urging mission-shapedness, authentic discipleship, and appropriate evangelism for today remains undiminished, passion and commitment we hope and pray you will increasingly come to share.

Pause...

Share with others those occasions when you look back on and see that God was at work in your life and shaped your life in specific ways. Who were the special people in your life who were God's agents?

What, for you, were the most significant assertions made in this chapter? Why?

Mission: God, the Church, and Evangelism

(For those who want to delve a bit deeper.)

In this chapter we introduce what we regard to be the two dominant understandings of Christian mission in recent decades and centuries—the *missio Dei* and the Great Commission. We explore their riches and appeal and some of the criticisms made of them. We outline our conviction that mission-shaped churches, fresh expressions of church, and evangelism advocated in this book, at their best inhabit and embody the best elements of both understandings of mission.

The very term *mission-shaped church* begs the question as to what the mission is that shapes such churches. "What is mission?" is a huge and complicated question, and there are many fine books addressing it specifically and deeply. Here we offer some basic contours.

The Mission of God—Missio Dei

For the last few decades, the term "mission" has been increasingly understood to relate first and foremost to the *mission of God* or *God's mission*, sometimes using the Latin phrase *missio Dei*. God—Father, Son, and Holy Spirit—is understood to be both the God *of* mission and God *on* mission. What Christian mission is and is like is made plain primarily by God's nature, activity, and intentions. Because ultimately, mission derives from God. It's God's idea before it's our idea. The word *missio* means "sent," and God the Holy Trinity is experienced as the Sender, Sent, and Sending One.

The Mission of God in the Scriptures

The essential source articulating the *missio Dei* is the Bible, and particularly the wonderful overarching story found throughout it—what John Wesley called the "grand truths" of scripture. God creates everything, and it is good. But even before the dew dries in paradise, humankind rejects

God's will and goes its own way. Yet God doesn't give up on rebel humanity. Time after time, God invites people to choose true life, through patriarchs and prophets, matriarchs and messengers, Torah and signs. Even when a parted sea, manna from heaven, and a living Law fail to restore humans to their God, God forges a new covenant, written on human hearts rather than tablets of stone. The means are many and varied, but the overall intentions and desires of God are clear.

Then, long foretold and when the time was right, the crucial part of God's mission takes shape. Jesus Christ, God self-sent as it were, takes human form and enters human history. In his living, dying, and rising, the Son undertakes the mission of redeeming all people and all creation to God. Through his teaching and healing, befriending and challenging, judging and forgiving, he makes God's priorities clear. Then God, in Christ, does what humanity can't do for itself. Dying, he destroys our death; and rising, he restores our life. On a full cross and by an empty tomb, God makes the way for all things to be forgiven, restored, and renewed.

The great story of scripture continues as Jesus Christ ascends to his native heaven and God the Holy Spirit falls upon and fills the fledgling communities of Christian believers. A missionary, self-sending God in action again, impelling and leading them outwards, from Jerusalem, Judea, and Samaria to the ends of the earth. God *among* them, urging and enabling the good news of salvation in Christ and the coming of God's kingdom in words and deeds. God *with* them, holding out the vision so vividly described at the end of the book of Revelation when all peoples from all places stand in awe and praise in the presence of God and God's Christ. A time when the leaves of the tree of life are for the healing of the nations, when there are no more tears or suffering, when the Lord Jesus Christ comes in glory and the mission of God fulfilled. From first to last, the Christian scriptures make known a God of mission and make plain the rich nature of God's mission.

Those persuaded of the *missio Dei* often express surprise that they never encountered this essential theme in scripture so loudly and clearly before they did. How could I have missed it, they say? Once your mission of God antennae is on, it's so obvious!

The Mission of God and the Coming of God's kingdom

Importantly, the *missio Dei* not only proposes the who and the what of Christian mission, but also its key *purpose.* This is, simply put, the coming of God's *kingdom,* the rule and reign of God, not just in the future there and then, but also in the present here and now. Jesus taught: "Your kingdom come, on earth as it is in heaven." God's mission is essentially about bringing the coming of God's kingdom to all, everywhere, in a rich palette of ways and means. At its best, the impetus and energy of mission-shaped churches, authentic reimagined evangelism, and all manner of fresh expressions of church is about joining the Spirit of God in this divine purpose.

> Pause...
>
> Share together the most helpful and relevant aspects of the missio Dei, for you and your local church at this point in time.

Before the Missio Dei

As we noted earlier, the *missio Dei* is a relatively recent understanding of mission, at least in terms of being formally identified and defined as such. So, the obvious question is, how was mission understood before that?

For much of Christian history, the word mission wasn't understood to refer primarily to *God's* nature and intentions, but rather the ministry and work of the *church* of Jesus Christ. Put simply, the church understood that it had been created, commanded, and commissioned by its Lord to the task of proclaiming the gospel and making disciples of Christ in all the earth. We see this in the Acts of the Apostles and throughout many centuries of Christian history in a bewildering variety of ways and means—not all of them very graceful or holy! Mission was what the church did to fulfil this task, often sending its agents to places where Christ and Christianity wasn't known with the aim of making him—and it—known. Where Christianity was established, becoming 'Christian' meant belonging to the Christian church in one of its proliferating versions, and believing and behaving as was deemed right by that church—and in some places and times, suffering the consequences if you didn't! But crucially, rather than understanding itself as primarily sharing in God's mission, the church understood itself to be the primary agent of mission, commissioned by Christ to represent its Lord on earth. For our purposes here, we will call this understanding of mission *the Great Commission*.

The Missio Dei and the Great Commission—Better Together

Sadly, there have been—and still are—churches, denominations, and organizations that choose either the *missio Dei* or *Great Commission* understanding of mission and the consequent understanding of the nature and role of the church, and largely reject the other. We are unable to do that. In advocating the need for more mission-shaped churches, more reimagined evangelism, more fresh expressions, and pioneering ministries we want and need both, believing that together, a better understanding of Christian mission is offered to the church today than either the *missio Dei* or *Great Commission* on their own can now provide. The remainder of this chapter explores this conviction.

> *Pause...*
>
> *Do you understand mission in primarily missio Dei terms, or Great Commission terms? Or perhaps both?*

Evaluating the Missio Dei

As we have begun to realize, one of the most important consequences of regarding mission as *missio Dei* is a different understanding of the status, role, and purpose of the *church*. Tim Dearborn, echoing both St. Augustine and Karl Barth, puts it like this: "It's not the church of God that has a mission in the world, but the God of mission who has a church in the world." Some think the significance of the church is reduced by understanding mission in terms of the *missio Dei* and if the church *itself* is regarded as being of supreme significance, it does. But as Roman Catholic scholars Bevans and Schroeder state at the start of their fine book *Constants in Context: Theology of Mission for Today*, "one of the most important things Christians need to know about the church is that *the church is not of ultimate importance*."[15] Those like us, who urge the need for mission-shaped church thinking and action agree. We believe that the church finds its true significance and role when it understands itself to be a *product* of God's mission, invited and intended by God to be a key *participant* and *partner* in God's mission. After all, Jesus didn't say, "seek first the church" but rather, "seek first the kingdom of God." Although the church is rightly the recipient of many grand titles found in the New Testament (like the Body of Christ and the People of God), it isn't an end in itself but a key vehicle to a greater end. Consequently, it can't ever truly be a turned in on itself thing because God has created it for essentially turned outwards kingdom purposes. Jesus didn't call his church into being, establish its ministries, and anoint its worship, then step back proudly and say, "Done. Mission accomplished!" The church is called into being by God through the work of Christ and empowered by the Holy Spirit to offer itself to God's mission in God's world. Just as Jesus, God's Son did—unto death if necessary.

There is a problem however. There is little evidence that accepting the idea of the *missio Dei* inevitably leads a church congregation to understand itself in these terms and live as if it were created for these purposes. Despite decades of explicit and implicit acceptance that mission is God's mission and the church is God's chosen partner in that mission, many local churches remain resistant or apparently impervious to understanding themselves in this way. Indeed, it is undeniable that during the decades when *missio Dei* thinking has been the most common way of understanding mission there has been a significant and lasting decline in

---

[15] Stephen Bevans and Roger Schroeder, *Constants in Context: A Theology of Mission for Today* (London: Orbis Books, 2003).

Christian believing and church belonging, in the West, and more recently in several other parts of the world. How can this be?

One possible explanation is that the *missio Dei* is so richly encompassing that it allows virtually everything a church does—whether church locally, regionally, or nationally—to be understood as mission. Caring for God's fragile planet and supporting a multitude of humanitarian and just causes. Seeking good ecumenical and interreligious relationships. Sustaining quality worship. Commitment to prayer and volunteering for a charity. Hosting neighborhood projects and being zealous about recycling. Forming a group to pick up local litter or build a school in a poverty-stricken country. Contributing to the local homeless hostel, food bank, thrift store, and the new church hall fund. Running a discipleship nurture course and inviting a guest preacher. And so on. Mission includes all this and more because God is known and experienced as encompassing and caring, profoundly committed to this earth and all its peoples. God urges love, justice, mercy, and peace. So whenever the church is engaged in these things, it is engaging in the *missio Dei*. What's the problem?

The problem is not that this rich and deep understanding of mission is wrong, but rather that identifying almost everything and anything as mission can equal nothing *specific* at all. The very encompassing nature of the *missio Dei* can produce bland rather than cutting-edge mission praxis. Ironically, it sometimes seems to disable rather than enable mission practice. It permits some churches to hide behind a nominal status quo and not engage in discerning the vital aspects of mission needed to become more potent vehicles of God's mission. Stephen Neill, a great historian of Christian missions famously commented, "If everything is mission, then nothing is mission, and we are back in the night in which all cats are grey." This caused Chris Wright, from the Oxford Centre for Mission Studies to disagree, writing, "If everything is mission . . . *everything is mission*." Nevertheless, the quandary remains that if virtually everything that a church does can be defined as mission then is the *missio Dei* simply whatever *the church chooses to do*? Is the church tail wagging the divine dog, so to speak? Just as some nineteenth century liberal theologians were charged with making Jesus in their own image, do some churches employ the *missio Dei* (whether knowingly or not) to endorse the dull and somewhat complacent life of their congregational clubs? We have both experienced local Methodist churches engaging in often extensive and expensive processes leading to the adoption of new mission and vision statements, the outcome of which is to continue everything it already does, end nothing it does, start nothing new and commit to no changes at all—except replacing an outdated notice board! Maybe!

It was Lesslie Newbigin (particularly during and after his roles in the *World Council of Churches* and its *Commission on World Mission and Evangelism*) who discerned a connection between understanding mission as everything we already do with resistance to change, complacency, and resulting inertia in many churches. He asserted this was a major issue for western Christianity, though there are growing signs that this is not merely a condition of churches in the West. Newbigin's response was to suggest that while there is a mission *dimension* to everything the church does, not everything the church does has a mission *intention*. Yet without such intention, he argued, the primary *purpose* of the *missio Dei* is misunderstood, whether innocently because of ignorance, or consciously because of complacency, bewilderment, resistance, and rejection.

Those like us, committed to mission-shaped church, reimagined evangelism, and fresh expressions urge the vital need for *intentionality*. We suggest that every church, of every size and type, in every place, must work out how it *best* engages in the *missio Dei*. This involves prayer and discernment, openness to biblical and theological insights, intelligent evaluation of the life of the church, of its congregations, neighborhood, and broader socio-political contexts. It involves readiness to change, to strategize and prioritize. It's less about a church rehearsing all its activity and service and congratulating itself for doing so many good and useful things and more about an act of obedience by Christ's disciples for whom discerning what God wants of them, wants to do with, and wants to do through them is the most important thing of all.

Other criticisms of the *missio Dei* have been made, but only one need concern us here. It is the serious assertion that primary emphasis on the *missio Dei* has sometimes divided Christians rather than united them.

Particularly that it is associated with types of theological liberalism and anti-evangelicalism. Sadly, there is some evidence for this, in both the recent past and the present times. As we have noted, the encompassing nature of the *missio Dei* and its commitment to God's kingdom coming permits and includes—even encourages—ecological, humanitarian and politicized activities in the name of Christ. For the large majority of Christians, this is not a problem in itself. Rather, the problem is that some of the Christians and churches who readily allow mission to be very many things, question the acceptability of evangelism and dismiss the value of Christian missions in earlier times.

While recognizing the force of these assertions—which we address briefly—we are strong advocates of a "both and" rather than an "either or" position. The *missio Dei* holds within it rich, diverse, and wonderful mission themes which are vitally important to every church, not least those seeking to be more profoundly mission-shaped. Crucially, it offers an adequate understanding of mission in a world of increasingly plural, multi-faith, no formal-faith, and secularized contexts. However, we want to assert that the *missio Dei* necessarily includes evangelism—meaning proclamation, conversion, and disciple-making. All these, like other aspects of the *missio Dei,* are rightly subject to evaluation, to developing understandings, practices, and applications. But they can't be disregarded or abandoned, and when attempts are made to do so, then Christian mission is a poorer, less complete thing than the *missio Dei* permits, enables, and demands—hence our repeated advocacy for new, reimagined, appropriate, and authentic evangelism.

Pause...

"We suggest that every church, of every size and type, in every place, must work out how it best engages in the missio Dei ..."

How does your church best engage in the missio Dei? Is it intentional about mission and evangelism? Begin to work it out.

The Great Commission

What of mission understood primarily as Great Commission? Christ's commanding and commissioning of his disciples to go and make disciples of all nations rooted in Matthew 28:16-20—rather than the broader, richer Commissions of Christ we outlined earlier—evolved over time into a belief that the church was to be the key agent of Christian mission. This was the broad understanding of mission that birthed the overseas mission movements of numerous Protestant Churches starting in earnest in the eighteenth century. Historically, it undergirded a hugely successful era of Christian expansion that lasted until the early twentieth century, at which point the 'sending' churches of the West started to decline just as many of the countries to which they had gone began to grow their own, often vibrant churches.

Reasons Not To?

It's important to note that prior to this age of modern missions, the idea of being commissioned by Christ was *less* prominent in church thinking. Reformers like Martin Luther and John Calvin shared a common view that the Great Commission of Jesus recorded in Matthew 28:18-20 was given only to the first disciples, rather than all disciples who came after them. This is one reason why a young Englishman, William Carey, had to argue the case with senior Baptists that it was the duty of all Christians to spread the gospel throughout the world and urged a commitment to overseas missions.

On that famous occasion in the 1790s a senior minister interrupted Carey, reportedly saying, "Young man, sit down. When God pleases to convert the heathen, he will do it without your aid and mine." This attitude to mission remains alive and well in many churches today. Then as now, some churches decide (whether through a conscious process of reflection or merely so as not to be inconvenienced) that it's God's responsibility to accomplish what God wants and that God doesn't need an agency like the church to effect God's purposes. After all, they say, God created all things (including humans) without their help—so God surely doesn't need us to transform the world? The church isn't *required* to be engaged in mission or evangelism.

You will not be surprised to learn that advocates of mission-shaped church hold to a different opinion. Whether mission is understood to be the *missio Dei* or the *Great Commission,* it's hard to contend that the church has no key role to play. While it may be the case that God doesn't *need* the church in the strict sense of being unable to effect kingdom purposes without it, both these key understandings of mission make clear that is simply not the way God operates. God delights to invite humans to share in the mission, in which there is a special and unique role and responsibility for the church of Christ. Consequently, it's a plainly incredible assertion on the part of the Christian church that it hasn't an active part to play in the missionary, kingdom purposes of God. Or indeed that it has the ability and right to choose not to be evangelistically mission-shaped!

Pause...

Consider: Do the activities and programs of your church indicate that it has or hasn't an active part to play in the mission of God?

Do you think your church has "the ability and right to choose not to be evangelistically mission-shaped"?

William Carey carried the day in the sense that his was a key voice persuading Christians of *their* responsibility to *go and make disciples of all nations.* What arose soon after however wasn't so much mission-shaped *churches* but missionary *societies*: the Baptist Missionary Society founded in 1792 being one of the first of hundreds. This is important because the church did then what it still so often does. It doesn't become mission-shaped *itself* as much as send missionaries or evangelists in its name or donate money so someone else can do the work. Mission, whether in Africa, Asia, and many places elsewhere in the early nineteenth century, or in the local church neighborhood today is regarded to be for those who like that sort of thing. Everyone else need not become involved, it's okay to outsource, to opt out.

Yet again, mission-shaped church advocates urge a different understanding. We point out that although mission societies did fantastic work—making Christians, founding schools and hospitals, building chapels and mission stations, and the like—it took them too long to give leadership and autonomy to indigenous peoples, and crucially too long to permit churches to be planted and grow in native soil—fresh expressions of church in new cultural contexts rather than mission stations of exported, largely western Christianity. Mission-shaped churches and fresh expressions are necessarily highly incarnational, and contextual. Ultimately, mission can't be outsourced in the sense that the church gives the task to others to undertake on its behalf. This isn't to suggest that all charities, para-church, and not-for-profit mission organizations should be abandoned by churches. But it is to suggest that alongside using their expertise's, mission-shaped churches are *themselves* mission-shaped, not merely churches supportive of mission. And there's a crucial difference between the two.

Pause...

Is yours a mission-shaped church in the sense that you raise money for mission organizations and charities and send it to them? Is it also itself mission-shaped?

Discuss.

Mission and Evangelism

You may have noticed that most of the material we are using to explore the *Great Commission* understanding of mission comes from what western sending countries used to call overseas mission. It's important to briefly explain why this is as it impacts mission-shaped church thinking today. The command of Christ was to go and make disciples of all nations. This requires that those who are Christian disciples go to those who aren't (yet) his disciples. But once Christianity was deemed to be established in a region or country, perhaps adopted as the official (main) faith of a society or nation, it was assumed to be a Christian country and therefore was no longer the object of Christian mission. A Christian country sent missionaries; it didn't receive them. (Except in terms of Catholics being sent to Protestant Christian regions, and vice versa.)

An older distinction between mission and evangelism may help us here. At the time of John Wesley, mission was generally understood as we have just described it, an activity among those not (yet) Christian; whereas evangelism was understood as an activity seeking to revive and deepen the Christian faith of an already Christianized region or nation. So, apart from his short and none-too-successful time as a missionary in Savannah, Georgia (a ministry which was itself largely exercised among European Christian settlers and colonists) John Wesley is generally regarded as an evangelist. However, his ministry in Britain, Ireland, and elsewhere beg questions of this easy distinction. For it is in such Christian countries that the Wesley brothers recognized that large numbers of people have no active or real Christian faith and make it their life's work to offer Christ to all. As part of this aim, they founded and supported numerous activities in Christian England that would be clearly understood to be mission rather than evangelism had they occurred in eighteenth century Africa. In short, mission and evangelism are not easy to neatly disentangle—then, or now.

Mission and Evangelism—Not Somewhere Else, but Here and Right Now

Advocates of mission-shaped churches are not alone in pointing out that we are in profoundly different cultural contexts today to anything previously existing. We have noted the decline of Christian faith and influence in the West, a loss of confidence in traditional evangelism to reach contemporary people, and the rise of "unbelief" of various kinds among our increasingly plural, secularized, no-faith, and multi-faith populations. Taken together these present a crucial piece of learning for those committed to mission-shaped church and reimagined evangelism. It is this: we now *all* live in places and spaces where the best practices of *both* 'mission' and 'evangelism' are required. Mission is no longer (if it ever really was) somewhere else. It's right here and right now. That's why mission-shaped churches not only 'send' but realize they are 'sent'. It's a key reason why mission-shaped churches are so vitally needed today.

Pause . . .

What do you think are the differences and similarities of "mission" and "evangelism"?

Do you consider your church is in a "missionary context" where it is currently situated?

Evaluating the Great Commission

The Great Commission understanding of mission, based on Matthew 28:16-20 has, like the *missio Dei,* been the subject of criticism and evaluation in recent times. Granted, it has been around much longer so there's more to chew over. What fulfilling the Great Commission means has been a long and involved debate. Some have placed the emphasis on reaching previously unreached peoples, posing the question at what point someone is deemed to be sufficiently reached for the Great Commission to be said to have been completed. Is it when a population can hear a radio program or watch a TV broadcast? When Christians go and preach to such peoples? When Christians live among, befriend, and create church with such peoples? When church buildings appear? Is it sufficient to make converts, or is it necessary to make disciples, and what's the difference? Then there are those who claim that the very notion of going and making disciples is passé and needs to stop. It is, they say, inevitably associated with collusion, manipulation, and expansion—just what the world doesn't need today. Others, including some from the economically poorer two-thirds world, point out that going and making disciples has a long and unholy relationship with colonialism and cultural imperialism. Missionaries themselves were almost all well-intentioned but inevitably presented the gospel, discipleship of Christ, and church style in the wrappings of a particular culture—most often capitalism, the quaint decorum of Victorian England, the cultural vitality of a diverse Europe, or the pioneering spirit of America. Perhaps because of such reasons, plus a growing sense of guilt contributing to a crisis of confidence, many in the West have given up on the idea of going and making disciples. Nowadays the large majority of missionaries and evangelists are non-western, and go to everywhere, including the West, and they suggest that the very decline of the Western church lies in part in its abandonment of heeding and obeying the Great Commission of Christ.

We are perhaps now more able to understand why some who embrace the *missio Dei* understanding of mission relegate or even abandon key aspects of mission and evangelism associated with the *Great Commission*. In comparison with their understanding of the *missio Dei,* the Great Commission carries the most baggage and the least perceived usefulness for the complex present and daunting future facing the Christian church, particularly (but increasingly not only) in the West.

Reimagining Evangelism and Mission

Like many advocates of mission-shaped church and new and reimagined evangelism, we are not unaware of the baggage associated with mission understood in terms of the Great Commission. However, we resist calls for it to be abandoned, and instead urge for its reimagining. Throughout this book are hints and clues as to what a reimagined "great commission" (set within a wider understanding of mission as God's mission and enriched by identifying great commissions in all four Gospels) might look like, be like, and feel like. Such an understanding of contemporary mission and evangelism lies at the heart of mission-shaped churches and fresh expressions. We offer a few "taster" themes here.

- The "body language" of the church, and what it speaks of is vitally important.
- Mission today is less about taking over and more about giving over and partnering with.

- Embodying Christ, and doing God's kingdom, is better than simply talking about it.
- Servanthood, forging mutually enriching partnerships and offering non-proprietorial hospitality are key.
- We must continue to go, recognizing that there are different ways of going but some are better than others. We should choose the better ways.
- Common witness marked by praise and gratitude to God, integrity of life, and gentle invitation is better than signals of superiority, veiled threats about ultimate destiny, and spelling out rules.
- The practical spirituality of Christianity is as important as its creeds in relation to good mission and evangelism.
- Discipleship of Christ is explored and pursued together, not done to some by others.

Pause...

Talk through this list of "taster themes." Which do you consider the most important (and challenging) to the life and witness of your church at this time?

John Wesley desired to restore what he called 'primitive Christianity', by which he meant the Christianity and the church in the early centuries of the faith as he understood it—specifically the Apostolic and Patristic ages. In significant part, Methodism came about as it did in consequence of this desire. So, we feel in good company when we point out that many valuable clues about mission-shaped church and evangelism reimagined for today come from the earlier centuries of Christianity—a time before medieval Christendom shaped and ruled the societies of much of the known world. A time long before the rifts and wars arising from the Reformation and responses to it. A long time prior to eighteenth century mission societies developing their own versions of going and making disciples. A time before Matthew 28:18-20 became known as the Great Commission or mission was identified in terms of the *missio Dei*. We can easily romanticize the early church, but when it was without much power, where it was a minority, when it lacked resources, where its reliance on God and the truth of the gospel were a crucially necessity, it has much to teach us today. Increasingly so, as the churches to which we ourselves belong move further into post-Christian contexts which resonate more profoundly with that of the early church than more recent eras in several influential ways.

Having briefly outlined and evaluated the *missio Dei* and *Great Commission,* we note one last, significant thing. Neither understanding of mission gives any encouragement to churches to opt out from or dismiss the call to become increasingly shaped by and for God's mission. The reverse is true. Every encouragement is given to churches to become ever more mission-shaped. But we know too that churches cannot and should not be bullied into choosing to become mission-shaped, and that *the* most significant realization is that becoming mission-shaped is what our wonderful God desires and wants for us—Christ's people, his church. Realizing this is a start of a congregational journey that is exciting, daunting, challenging, costly, and anointed.

We make no apologies for banging the mission-shaped drum. Long experience suggests that it takes a considerable time for mission-shapedness—and a (re)commitment to appropriate and authentic evangelism as a key part of that—to become accepted, embedded, and instinctive in local churches. When we don't regularly rehearse together who we are and what God desires and wants of us, *and* continually reconfigure our life as church in consequence of it, then we quickly and repeatedly revert to a former life as church which tends to misshape us. We who occupy ordained and lay leadership roles discover (sometimes to our surprise) that we keep exercising our ministries in terms opposite to the commands of Jesus. He said, "I will build my church," and we spend most of our time and talents striving to build the church. He said, "go and make disciples" and we stay put, expecting him (or someone other than us) to do that. John Wesley famously said, "I regard the whole world as my parish." Sadly, his successor Methodists often appear to passively regard their congregational parish as their whole world. They are not alone in this. Converts to mission-shaped church thinking and action urge all of us not to forget who is who, and what is what. We need courage to keep remembering the primacy of the mission of God and the commission of Christ, if only because when we don't, we slip quickly back into church for its own sake and church for our sake mode, in which there is no real future.

Those like us, committed to the essential missional nature of the church and the need for ever more varied fresh expressions and reimagined evangelism are sometimes accused of being negative and overly critical of local churches, of running them down, and never being satisfied. If you get this impression in these pages, please forgive us. We don't dismiss or take lightly the significance of worship offered humbly and faithfully to God, the power of presence and witness over many years, the service of others graciously offered in a myriad of ways, the profound worth of fellowship and care, the ministry at the key points of human life, and the generosity, kindness, and loyalty we find in so many churches. The call to become mission-shaped isn't primarily a call to *do* more to bring about yet more exhaustion in the often workhouse environment of the local church. It's more a call to each church (local, regional and denominational) to place itself at the use and disposal of a God of mission. This often requires a church to make hard choices: a readiness to change, taking on new things while laying other things down, even honestly working out whether or not they have a future, then planning accordingly. The words and sentiment of the Methodist Covenant prayer, usually said by disciples standing together in worship is most appropriate for church congregations, not only individuals:

> We are no longer our own but yours.
> Put us to what you will . . .
> We freely and wholeheartedly yield all things
> to your pleasure and disposal

Becoming More Evangelistically Mission-Shaped: A Methodist, Wesleyan Perspective

(Especially for those for whom Christian tradition is significant and formative—but not only them.)

We are both Methodist pastors and consequently (like anyone else deep rooted in a Christian tradition) speak think most naturally from within and out of that tradition. We are also pastors in Church denominations that, at least in our own native United States and Great Britain, are in a state of some decline and are prayerfully (even desperately) seeking their way under God. In this chapter we explore and advocate various mission-shaping themes which we believe belong firmly within our Methodist tradition and Wesleyan heritage, which sometimes give a particular 'mood' and 'tone' to themes which belong to the whole Church of Christ. We begin with grace, which gives us hope.

Abundant Grace and Liberating Hope

It's hard to overstate the significance of God's grace in Wesleyan theology and practice. In his book, *Practical Divinity*, Thomas Langford offers a reflection on the grace of God:

> In a basic sense, grace is Jesus Christ. Grace is the specific expression of God's nature and will, an incarnate and continuing presence. From the *center in Jesus Christ*, implications radiate, ranging from the prevenient grace of God to justification, regeneration, assurance, sanctification, means of grace and final glorification. The grace of God, expressed in and defined by Jesus Christ, becomes inclusive of life.[16]

---

[16] Thomas Langford, *Practical Divinity: Theology in the Wesleyan Tradition* (Nashville: Abingdon Press, 1998), 41.

Around this point—*the grace of God in Jesus Christ*—several attendant commitments form a tight nexus: biblical witness to Jesus Christ, vital experience of God in Christ as Savior and Sanctifier, commitment to human freedom and ethical discipleship, and the shaping of church life around missional responsibility.[17]

The Wesleyan tradition has always understood the pathway towards salvation as being resourced by the gift of God's abundant grace. This grace is known to us in the following ways:

Prevenient Grace is the presence of God in all people, prior to our acceptance of faith or conscious response to divine revelation. We believe that every person is created in God's image, that all persons are of 'sacred worth,' that no one is outside of God's love and saving activity. These theological convictions, deep rooted in the Wesleyan tradition, result in commitments to ministries with and among all peoples. This has global implications. For example, it resonates with the Revised Preamble to the Constitution of the Uniting Church in Australia, that "the First Peoples had already encountered the Creator God." Going more deeply into the thought of John Wesley himself, this is stated explicitly in his "Thoughts Upon Slavery." It is important, when we move into public spaces (as representative lay and clergy ministers of the gospel) to remember that we do not take the grace of God into these spaces. God's 'going before us' grace is already present.

Justifying Grace is the gift of salvation, which is ours through faith and apart from any merit. The ground is indeed level at the foot of the cross. We are saved by God's grace because of faith. This salvation is God's gift. It's not something we possess. It's not something we did of which we can be proud (Ephesians 2). Fleming Rutledge speaks of an active God who is "binding himself in an unconditional covenant, revealing himself in the calling of a people, self-sacrificing in the death of his Son, prodigal in the gifts of the Spirit, justifying the ungodly, and, indeed, offending

---

[17] Langford, *Practical Divinity*, 250.

the "righteous" by the indiscriminate use of [God's] favor."[18] The assurance that we can trust in the faithfulness of God through Jesus Christ to save us from sin (Romans 5) was a strong emphasis in the Reformed tradition which led to the English phrase "justified by faith"—one of the traditions that shaped the Wesleyan heritage.

Sanctifying Grace is the journey toward holiness. This is our lifelong response to divine grace. At this point, our divisions become evident. Some emphasize personal (or interior, or cloistered) holiness, the inward journey. Others value social justice, the reign of God with all of its public and structural implications. The former sometimes see holiness through the lens of personal purity or piety; the latter through the consequences of how it transforms communities and liberates those Jesus names, for example in Luke 4. And of course, holiness, or grace, is not bifurcated: Wesley spoke most often of sanctification as the love of God *and* neighbor.

God's grace is abundant. To flatten grace is to cheapen it. To restrict grace is to deny its very essence. Grace is a gift to us, but certainly a gift to be shared, lest our being called and chosen looks more like mere privilege (Isaiah 42). Thus grace, by its very nature, overflows the banks of our own streams into the *oikos*, the great household and the vast ecosystem that sustains and includes us all. And this is the basis for a hope that liberates. This liberation finds expression most powerfully in the Wesley hymn—"My chains fell off, my heart was free!"

Conversation about grace and hope, if it is to resonate, must take into account the real lives of those we know and serve, the real lives of those who share in this common life.

Pause…

In what ways are these facets of divine grace discernible in your local church today?

---

[18] Fleming Rutledge, Generous Orthodoxy, sermons. htpps://generous orthodoxy.org.

This leads to a key question.

> How might the Church bear witness in public spaces to
> God's abundant grace and liberating hope, made plain in the
> reconciling love and compassion of Christ?

We believe this involves several overlapping and evolving, mission-potent processes.

Diagnosing the Present Reality

Ken writes:

A few years ago, I fell on the steps of a convention center stage. I quickly realized I couldn't get up. I was surrounded immediately by friends who took me to the nearest Emergency Room. There, I was seen by the staff and x-rays were taken. They revealed no broken bones, so the remainder of the day was an exercise in the staff's trying to release me, and my corresponding inability to stand in my own strength. As the hours went by, they gave me more and more medication thinking this would mask the pain. My wife finally assured them that I was not a person who was inclined to want to stay in a hospital unless it was absolutely necessary. A staff member asked me to lift my leg. I could not. "Oh," he said, and I was wheeled to a room for the night. The MRI, taken the next morning, revealed a ruptured quad tendon and surgery was scheduled for the next day.

So, which comes first? Treatment or diagnosis?

In The Practice of Adaptive Leadership, Heifetz, Linsky, and Grashow of the Harvard Business School write: "In most organizations, people feel pressure to solve problems quickly, to move to action. So, they minimize the time spent in diagnosis, collecting data, exploring multiple possible interpretations of the situation and alternative potential interventions"[19]

There are several probable reasons why this is so in our congregations, as in other places. We have limited time and space (like an ER). We want to reduce or eliminate the pain quickly. We think all problems benefit from the same solution. We think the answer is simple, and therefore too much thought is unnecessary.

The art of diagnosis is both iterative and itinerant, as we are "moving back and forth among data collection, interpretation and action"[20] In the leadership of pastoral and missional ministry, we don't have the luxury of being in an ivory tower, separated from those with whom we live and serve. From the days of Francis Asbury in eighteenth century America—or we go could further back to a Francis of Assisi in twelfth century Italy—we too are "iteratively itinerant," and it is from this that we are exposed to the various data that forms the basis of our diagnosis. The data that we collect is in the metrics, the stories, the profiles, the visits, the phone calls, the emails, the letters, the history that we celebrate, the history we would rather suppress, the long-term trends, and the conversations we have with each other. But it is also in the listening to God, the silence, the study of scripture, the mission contexts that surround a local church, and the people in the community who are not in the church. As we resist the urge to fix or act too quickly, we are seeking to avoid treatment without an appropriate diagnosis. Heifetz and his co-authors are clear: "The single most important skill and most undervalued capacity for exercising adaptive leadership is diagnosis."

---

[19] Ronald Heifetz, Alexander Grashow, and Marty Linsky, *The Practice of Adaptive Leadership: Tools and Tactics for Changing Your Organization and the World* (Brighton: Harvard Business Press, 2009), 7.

[20] Heifetz, Grashow, and Linsky, *The Practice of Adaptive Leadership*, 7.

So, in response to the question, "Which comes first—diagnosis or treatment?" Diagnosis comes first—always.

> *Pause...*
>
> *What might "taking diagnosis seriously" mean for your congregation, as you reflect on your life together?*

For those of us who might be prone to treat the body, we do not dare suppress those voices who ask the provocative questions that lead us to diagnose what is really going on. Where, for example, in the life of the church, is abundant grace? And where is liberating hope?

We can assess the present reality in many of our local churches (in North American, British, and European Christianity) and acknowledge that we need to reach more people, younger people, and more diverse people—to borrow language of Lovett Weems. If we do not find them in large numbers in our assemblies or sanctuaries, we might ask what the encounter of abundant grace and liberating hope will look like in our public spaces? And what is the most essential spiritual practice in those contexts?

Practicing the Art of Diagnosis through Listening

Fresh Expressions are forms of church which come into being through *listening, witness, service, incarnational mission,* and intentionality about *making Christian disciples.*

A deacon in Florida was describing his church's partnership with the schools and especially the at-risk children in the surrounding community, and said, "we begin with a questioning model." A questioning model implies that we don't begin with answers, but with listening. What are people thinking and feeling? What conversations are going on in their minds and hearts? Of course, our listening to others is deepened as we have been listening to God. Dietrich's Bonhoeffer made this point with characteristic passion in his little book, *Life Together*: "Many people are looking for an ear to listen. They do not find it among Christians, because these Christians are talking where they should be listening. But the one who can no longer listen to his brother or sister will soon be no longer listening to God."[21] Bonhoeffer goes on to describe love for God as listening to God's word, and love for our neighbor as listening to them.

Fresh Expressions literature sometimes uses the term 'third places', borrowed primarily from sociology. Third places are settings where listening to each other can occur—a coffee shop, diner, or pub. Both of us love sport—Ken the American sport of baseball and Martyn the game of cricket which originated in England. Both are games of slow pace, some duration, and consequently permit ample time to talk with friends (or even strangers) to catch up on where we've been, how things are, and what's going on in the world. In contrast, technological devices (as helpful and bewilderingly clever as they are) don't help us in the experience of really listening to each other. There's an absence of embodiment; we are not really physically present with each other. And so many have come to the practice of setting all such devices aside at meals, putting them in silent mode for other conversations to take place, or turning them off after a certain time in the evening. Have no fear; everything will be captured and available when we return!

Serving in dynamically multi-cultural Florida, Ken is committed to an ongoing process of improving his Spanish. One way of doing this is to try to speak it when with a friend for whom it is their first language. Another way is to ask native Spanish speakers to speak slowly to each other and try to follow what they are saying. Still another is to read the Bible in Spanish, especially the Psalms. One word that appears over and over again in the Psalms is *escuchar*, to listen. We listen to God: *escucha a Dios*. We ask God to hear our prayers: *escucha mi oracion*. We listen to each other. Another common word is *buscar*, to seek, to search. *Estoy*

---

[21] Deitrich Bonhoeffer, *Life Together: The Classic Exploration of Christian in Community* (Harper One, 1978) 97–98.

buscando la scripturas, I search the scriptures. We seek and search for God; God seeks and searches for us; and we seek and search for each other and for the lost. Listening is wrapped up in seeking and searching for each other: who we really are and what is really going on. We begin with a questioning model.

Jesus used the questioning model expertly. Teaching in an iterative way, he constantly posed questions to his disciples and followers:

- Who do you say that I am?
- What does it profit us to gain the world and forfeit our lives?
- Do you know what I have done to you?
- Are you able to drink the cup that I drink?
- When was it that we saw you sick or in prison and visited you?
- And perhaps, one of the most profound questions in all of scripture, found in Jesus' parable of the Good Samaritan: Who is my neighbor?

This question was posed in response to the Law that he and we know very well—that we love our neighbor. It's a very appropriate question. And of course, listening is a form of love. To question is to begin with the assumption that God and grace are already present in a person's life. It is a reciprocal relationship of giving and receiving. Public discourse in both the United States and the United Kingdom in recent times is marked by a lack of listening to each other, of often assuming the worst about each other, or that we already know all there is to know. This is our impasse, in the church and in our wider cultures.

Pause...

Who does your congregation listen to, and who is ignored?

In what ways does your church adopt a questioning, listening model rather than an informing, instructing model?

Such Listening Implies a Convicted Humility

We are in need of a convicted humility and a shared repentance. A convicted humility implies that we have convictions—beliefs and perspectives that anchor us in a place and in relation to the world—and that we hold these convictions with some degree of lightness. We do so because, in the words of the Apostle Paul, we see through a glass darkly, (1 Corinthians 13). Which is to say that we are not all-knowing, and everything has not been fully revealed to us. The tagline in one United States denomination that "God is still speaking" is intended to push against the idea of a closed canon; we listen for the conviction of the Holy Spirit, who will guide us into all of the truth (John 17).

And yet, God's corrective speech is not (merely) turned toward others, among those persons we perceive to be not as open-minded as we imagine ourselves to be, but is also turned toward ourselves. Here a convicted humility must lead to a shared repentance.

When we see ourselves as we really are, we can see the world as it really is. And one of the learnings of this contemplation is that we are not separate from the world. We are not 'in here' and the world is not 'out there'. For better or worse, we are connected, bound together, in the words of Martin Luther King Jr., in "an inescapable network of mutuality."[22] The benefit of this is that it works against our sense of isolation; the challenge is that it is humbling.

How can people of faith become better known as people who really listen? To God? And to our neighbors? And *where* might we undertake these spiritual practices?

> Pause . . .
>
> *To what extent is our discipleship of Christ, and that of our congregations, marked by careful listening and convicted humility?*
>
> *Where might we best undertake these spiritual practices?*

---

[22] Martin Luther King Jr., *Letter from a Birmingham Jail* (1963).

Being Incarnationally Present in Public Spaces

The processes of diagnosis and discernment, particularly for disciples and spiritual leaders in our time, occur within the necessary movement of ministry. There is a need to find the deserted places (Mark 1: 35) where we might hear the still, small voice (I Kings 19). There is the ordering of life that includes both action and contemplation. This needs to include the practice of what Heifetz and his colleagues term "getting on the balcony,"[23] where we gain some distance and perspective from the day-to-day work of oversight and ministry, which is the dance we find ourselves in. For some, the balcony is a different geographical location (a cabin in the mountains or by a lake). For others, it is a day in a park or a few hours of solitude in a favorite coffee venue.

But diagnosis and discernment also take place in the 'murky waters' of the events and relationships of one's ministry. Here reflection happens in the midst of action: as one is leading a meeting, mediating conflict, preaching a sermon, or counseling someone. In the moment we are called to weigh an option, to interpret a situation, to suggest a way forward. The best coaches and mentors know that these settings are often better for the asking of additional questions than the definition of answers, and yet the conversations themselves are helpful.

Danny Morris and Chuck Olsen note three contexts that are especially fertile for discernment: [24]

- the closet (the individual)
- the house (a small group of trusted friends or colleagues)
- and the sanctuary (the public assembly)

Spiritual leaders both lay and ordained will recognize each evident in the ministry of Jesus—his early morning practice of retreat, his going apart with the inner circle of disciples, his public encounters with religious leaders. We too need to find and sustain a rhythm of diagnosis and

---

[23] Heifetz, Grashow, and Linsky, *The Practice of Adaptive Leadership*.

[24] Danny Morris and Charles Olsen, *Discerning God's Will Together: A Spiritual Practice for the Church* (Lanham: Rowman & Littlefield, 1997).

discernment in our own ministries—a healthy practice of quiet prayer, meditation and study; the reliance on a small group of confidants in whom we have great trust; and the public and inclusive spaces where the church often encounters the missional contexts and needs of its neighborhood. In its most mature expression, spiritual leadership will occur across all three of these contexts, and each is essential to the rest.

Pause...

Do we engage enough in diagnosis and discernment as individuals and congregations?

Do we pay sufficient attention to each of the three contexts?

Are we allowing the diagnosis and discernment coming from each context to resource and shape the others?

Identifying and Inhabiting "Third Places"

It will help to pay attention to the places where people increasingly gather and to be less generic but more particular about defining them. Sociologists, like Ray Oldenburg, call these "third places."[25] Imagine that the first two places are your home first, and your work second. What is your third place? For those of us belonging to a church culture, the third place was almost always the church. It was where you went to meet people, to help your children make friends, to play on a sports team, to make business connections, to be a meaningful part of the community, or to run for political office. The church has a presence in that culture, but increasingly it is more marginalized in most other contexts. What are our emerging third places today?

- Coffee shops
- Pubs and Breweries

---

[25] Ray Oldenburg, *Celebrating the Third Places: Inspiring Stories about the Great Good Places at the Heart of Our Community* (Boston: Da Capo Press, 2009).

- Arts Communities
- Political Organizations
- Sports Teams
- Digital Culture

And we could add to an increasingly long list.

If we are going to meet and engage more people, younger people, and more diverse people, we are required to be incarnationally present where people increasingly gather, not where we wish them to be. We need also to pay more attention to the networks that connect people, and less attention solely to neighborhoods. People form deep relationships not necessarily with those they live closest to, but increasingly with those with whom they share passions around intellectual life, recreation, politics, hobbies, games, media. And we could add to an increasingly long list.

> Pause...
>
> What are the most fertile 'third places' in relation to your local church?
>
> Where do people physically gather in your neighborhood—and around what interests and shared passions?
>
> In terms of the time and resources allocated to it by your local church, how important is both identifying and inhabiting 'third places'?
>
> Does it need a higher priority, and if so, how will you go about ensuring that happens?

Discipling Persons into the way of Jesus

Of course, the diagnosis, the listening, the incarnational presence is for the purpose of *making disciples*, or, more literally (Matthew 28: 19) to "disciple" (mathetes) others in the Christian faith. A common critique of 'making' disciples is that it can be seen as formulaic or mechanistic, as if the sole focus is our own agency. The error here is that disciples come into being through the Holy Spirit. Each new disciple is an outward and visible sign of God's abundant grace and liberating hope, not the product of our efficiency, ingenuity, or ability. Material on discipling, and the interplay between what only God can do, and what Christ's followers are charged to do, is found in several places throughout this book.

Pause...

To what extent do you believe that discipling people into the way of Jesus is something you should and could do?

What kind of prioritizing is discipling each other given in your church?

We reach a third key issue.

Bearing witness to God's grace in Christ through our life and mission?

Through a mixed economy of leadership for a mixed economy of church

As we've noted, the phrase "mixed economy" is traced to Archbishop Rowan Williams, who talked about new expressions of church alongside inherited (or parish) expressions of church[26] We might think of the church as it has existed, and the church as we see it in potential. Or the church we inherit versus the church we want to pass on to others. Or we might think of the church within the walls of our buildings and the church beyond the walls of our buildings.

This frame may be helpful:

- Attractional + Missional
- Tradition + Innovation
- The Church as Building + The Church as Community

---

[26] Rowan Williams, "Making the Mixed Economy Work" (Fresh Expressions National Day Conference, Oxford, May 6, 2011).

- The Church as Structure + The Church as Movement
- Inherited Church Models + Fresh Expressions

A mixed economy holds all of this together. It is not either/or, but rather both/and.

The word "economy" derives from the Greek word *oikos*. Oikos means house, household, and home. We might say that housekeeping includes resources of time, space, and money, and home is about boundaries of place, restorative space, and acceptance. Families are economic communities. Who does the laundry? Who prepares the meals? Who cares for the children? Who keeps the budget? And homes are deeply personal: think about your bed, your closet, household objects that were passed down to you.

So, when we begin to talk about a mixed economy of leadership, it is complex. But it is a much-needed conversation. We cannot have mixed economies of church without mixed economies of leadership, which rightly and inevitably includes laity at a profound level. Increasingly, a mixed economy of pastoral and missional leadership is essential—pastor-teachers, planters, pioneers and many others.

Pause...

Is there a mixed economy of leadership in your church?

Is your leadership sufficient to aid and resource a mixed economy of church in your contexts and neighborhood?

A mixed economy of leadership will draw upon an ancient source: a diversity of gifts.

Remembering There Is a variety of Spiritual Gifts

Now there are varieties of gifts (*charismata*), but the same Spirit; and there are varieties of services (*diakonia*), but the same Lord;

and there are varieties of activities (*energemata*), but it is the same God who activates all of them in everyone. (1 Corinthians 12: 4-6)

Paul speaks of the relationship between gifts, service, and energy. We are in our "sweet spot" when these dynamics form a triangle, strengthen, and support each other. We are at our best—we are fulfilling God's purpose in our lives and our callings when we hold these three together.

The word gift (*charismata*) is rooted in the New Testament Greek word for grace (*charis*). This reminds us that any gift that we might have is a gift of God's grace and not our achievement or merit. In her book *Retrieving Charisms for the Twenty-First Century*, Doris Donnelly wrote, "Charisms *are a special variety of gifts dispensed through the Holy Spirit in Church and world, as needed, for the common good.*"[27] This reminds us not only of the divine source of such gifts, but that they are given for *both* the world and church—not just the church—in response to need, for the common good, and most certainly not to produce self-important, smugly-superior disciples! Paul makes this point insisting that "To each is given the manifestation of the Spirit for the common good." (1 Cor 12:7)

The word *sympheron* (common good) comes from Greek and Roman politics and is related to coming together for mutual benefit. It is also a cognate of our word for symphony. How do we hear many voices, the pronounced and the muted voices? We are given spiritual gifts not for individual self-definition, but for others and to work together with others. Any person in any Christian ministry knows, even when they pretend otherwise, that this work is not about us. We do this work for others. We sit at these tables in order to see the gifts of others. And churches enter public spaces not to colonize them, but to seek the common good—in the language of Jeremiah, the *shalom* of the city. (Ch 29:4-13)

Accordingly, proper Christian spirituality is connected to service (*diakonia*). Bishop Pereira of the Methodist Church of Cuba tells how

---

[27] Doris Donnelly, *Retrieving Charisms for the Twenty-First Century* (Saint Joseph: Liturgical Press, 1999), 9.

during the revival in that church many would pray through the night to receive charismatic gifts. Once, two young men came to him and said, "We prayed all night, we have received the gift, now what do you want us to do?" He responded, "Now that you have received the gift of the Spirit, there is a mop, leaning against the wall. You could begin by cleaning the church!"[28]

Pause . . .

What is your gift? How are you serving? Where is your energy?

Recovering the Qualities of a Movement within Our Institutions.

Ken writes:

So, I went through surgery, on my ruptured quad tendon, then a summer of physical therapy. The therapist would work with me, and in the first stages that was to keep the leg straight to heal. But then one day he said to me, "Now we enter a different phase. We need to regain the range of motion." I needed to learn again how to do what I had once been able to do: bend and be flexible. I remembered the phrase "muscle memory", and I connected that with the church. How can we become a movement again? How can we be flexible? How can an institution regain a range of motion that allows it to be in life and ministry with new people, younger people, and more diverse people? How do we regain our strength, for the purpose of offering abundant grace and liberating hope? Again, suggested responses to such questions are offered throughout this book.

---

[28] Richard Pereira in discussion with the author.

Pause...

What would it mean for your local church to 'recover the qualities of a movement'?

Sustained by Abundant Grace—Resilient and Seeking Renewal in Liberating Hope

Andrew Zolli has defined resilience as "the capacity of a person, system or enterprise to maintain its core purpose and integrity in the face of dramatically changed circumstances."[29]

During the long, complex season of ministry during the first Covid 19 pandemic, Bishop Janice Huie led a retreat for a group of Methodist leaders to reflect on resilience. She posed a few key questions: [30]

- What is our core purpose?
- What does it mean for us to live with integrity?
- What are signs of our dramatically changed circumstances?

Those present came to better understand that the practice of resilience, as leaders, was closely related to their resilience as persons. How are we anchored spiritually? This is akin to the Wesleyan question: "How is it with our souls?" How we are participating in networks, again, as Wesleyans put it: "Are we watching over one another in love?" What is the health of our humility and our courage? In other words, the renewal of our institutions and our movement cannot be separated from our own personal and spiritual renewal.

So how do you take this away, based on who you are? How do you take all that you have learned, in your formation and the formation of

---

[29] Andrew Zolli and Ann Marie Healy, *Resilience: Why Things Bounce Back* (New York: Simon & Schuster Inc., 2013).

[30] Janice Huie, *Reservoirs of Resilience in Uncertain Times: Reflections on Hope, Courage, and Purpose* (Texas Methodist Foundation, December 21, 2020).

others in your local church, and how do you integrate this with your context?

How do you engage with problems, such as:

- I cannot be myself and be in ministry.
- We don't know who we are as a church.
- Our church is overcome by depression or grief which manifests itself as displaced anger.
- We are not connected with our community or context.

Here we use material in Martyn's book, *Resourcing Renewal,*[31] further developed and applied by Ken. This is a way of renewal and, more basically, a way of becoming disciples in the way of Jesus.

First: We Return to the Gospel (Identity)

- How do we return to the gospel each day?
- How do we live a life shaped by the mind of Jesus (which is both humility and courage)?
- What patterns and habits in the life of Jesus do we see?
- What core teachings of Jesus are at the heart of our calling?

Here is a *simple model* of returning to the gospel each day, based on design thinking. Of course, you might adapt it to your own spiritual practice.

- Immerse yourself in the gospel. Read a verse, a passage, or a chapter. Practice centering prayer. Imagine with the senses. Taste and see. Journal. Draw. Doodle.
- Expand your perceptions. Where did you see and become aware of Jesus in the past twenty-four hours? What are you most grateful for? What are you most anxious, fearful, or disturbed about?
- Design the day. What can you engage? What can you let go of? How can you share? How can meals be different? How can technology be different? How is friendship a part of your life?

---

[31] Atkins, *Resourcing Renewal,* 2010.

- Act on the gospel. What are one to three actions that are the most urgent? That will have the most impact? How might you imitate Christ in a small way?

Second: We Rediscover the Founding Charisms, or Charisms of the Founders (Purpose)

Recall the definition of Doris Donnelly: "Charisms are a special variety of gifts dispersed through the Holy Spirit in Church and world, as needed, for the common good."[32]

- Why do we exist as a church?
- What is distinctive about your particular branch of the Christian tradition?
- How does this distinctiveness contribute to the larger church's mission and witness in a community?
- How can we define and relate our doctrine of the church (ecclesiology) as the mission of the church (missiology)?

Here is a brief reflection from our shared Methodist tradition from the late Bishop Rueben Job:

Methodist life was marked by a deep and authentic personal piety that led to a broad and uncompromising social involvement. Methodists were known for their prayers and for their commitment to the poor and disenfranchised. This commitment resulted in persistent efforts to build houses of prayer and worship as well as consistent efforts to visit the prisons, build schools and hospitals, and work for laws which moved toward a just and peaceful social order. Not everyone agreed with or applauded the way early Methodists lived, but it did not require many at any one place to make a difference. Because they took their relationship to Jesus Christ with utmost seriousness, their life of prayer and witness was readily identified and often contagious as many wanted what Methodists appeared to have."

---

[32] Donnelly, *Retrieving Charisms for the Twenty-First Century* (1999), 9.

Among these Methodist gifts were a certain knowledge of their own salvation, and at-homeness in this world and confidence in the next, a living companionship with a living Christ, and access to the power of God that could and did transform the most broken and hopeless persons into productive, joyful and faithful disciples. Such was the power of God at work in the way Methodists lived. Methodists believed that they were to be the leaven that God could use to transform the church and the world.[33]

Pause...

Why do you think you were set apart, called into a role whether lay or ordained, to lead this particular community at this specific time?

Third: We Read the Signs of the Times (Context)

If we are spiritual leaders we are called to undertake the integrative work of diagnosis and discernment with great seriousness. The Lord, speaking through the prophet Jeremiah about the qualities of the prophets and priests in the sixth century B.C. gives voice to our crisis. "They have treated the wound of my people carelessly, saying peace, peace, when there is no peace" (Jeremiah 6: 14).

Spiritual leadership is of vital importance because there is a great deal at stake—in many communities the health of the faith community and its capacity to support and engage is the difference between life and death for many, especially children and youth.

One of the most significant models of diagnosis and discernment in the public sphere in the United States can be found in the ministry of William Barber, the pastor and activist from Goldsboro, North Carolina. In

---

[33] Rueben Job, *A Wesleyan Spiritual Reader* (Abingdon: Nashville, 1998), 193–94.

his memoir *The Third Reconstruction,*[34] he describes a process that leads to civil disobedience that includes:

- gathering data and fact
- an attempt to negotiate with those in power
- the self-purification that enters into a suffering that transforms enemies into friends
- direct action and acceptance of consequences

To read the signs of the times, in the language of Vatican II, is a complex art. We will become more collaborative, more conversant with the literature of adaptive change, and more immersed in the spiritual disciplines of our faith. This will require more, not less, from each of us—thus our need for resilience. And yet the massive human needs in the world alongside the fragile state of the church itself call for leadership and oversight (guidance, encouragement, and accountability) that incorporates the excellence of human wisdom, the depth of scripture, and the best of our traditions.

We believe a greater possibility of renewal comes when a local church open to the Holy Spirit addresses these three key issues of identity, purpose and context with courage and honesty.

Identity - The question, "Who are we?," which is rooted in a return to the gospel.

Purpose - The question, "Why are we here?," which is grounded in a rediscovery and reimagining of the founding charisms.

Context - The question, "When and where and how do we live?," which is based on our reading of the signs of the times.

Importantly, they are not meant to be understood in a linear way—separately addressing the first, then the second, etc. Rather let each inform and teach the others—the outcomes being greater then the sum of the parts.

---

[34] William Barber II and Jonathan Wilson-Hartgrove, *The Third Reconstruction: How a Moral Movement is Overcoming the Politics of Division and Fear* (Boston: Beacon Press, 2016).

Pause . . .

Should your local church set aside time to undertake this exercise of "resourcing renewal"?

If so, when?

Conclusion: A Confidence in the Gospel that is Abundant Grace and Liberating Hope

We conclude with a word from Vincent Donovan's memoir, *Christianity Rediscovered*, and the Prophet Isaiah.

"We are called to announce the good news of Jesus and trust that those of other cultures and generations will interpret it for themselves. Ours is to communicate, theirs is to respond. We must know the gospel and teach it, but not force our interpretations on others. We are tempted to align with political or economic systems, but these are not and can never be equated with the kingdom of God. Neither is the church the kingdom of God. The church is always on the way to the kingdom and is only a part of the mission of God."[35]

"The goal of evangelism is to place all things under the lordship of Jesus Christ. This is our destiny and the evangelist or pastor or missionary or witness is simply a channel of hope for those who do not have it. Leadership is not calling people back to where we once were, or where we ourselves are at the moment. Leadership is going with people, across generations and cultures, to a place neither they nor we have been before."[36]

And from Isaiah 41:17-20:

When the poor and needy seek water, and there is none, and their tongue is parched with thirst, I the Lord will answer them. I the Lord will not forsake them. I will open rivers on the bare

---

[35] Vincent Donovan, *Christianity Rediscovered* (Nashville: Orbis Books, 2003).

[36] Donovan, *Christianity Rediscovered*.

heights, and fountains in the midst of the valleys. I will make the wilderness a pool of water, and the dry land springs of water. I will put in the wilderness the cedar, the acacia, the myrtle and the olive; I will set in the desert the cypress, tech plane and the pine together, so that all may see and know, all may consider and understand, that the hand of the Lord has done this, the Holy One of Israel has created it.

God has called and chosen us, not for privilege, but to be a servant church in the public spaces where people are already present and seeking abundant grace and liberating hope. But in the service there is fatigue and fear: fatigue in the enormity of all that needs to be repaired in this world and fear in the prospect that we are not the people we imagine ourselves to be.

Yet the good news could not be more clearly stated; again and again the Lord says to us, "do not be afraid." God is with us. God is for us—to keep our feet from stumbling on the iterative way. How firm foundation a foundation, indeed.

So, in this season of scarcity, we believe that the Lord will relieve our fatigue with abundant grace. And in this season of much despair, we trust that God will remove our fears and provide liberating hope. This is the core of a Mission-Shaped Wesleyan Evangelism. And her scripture and tradition flow towards each other in dialogue, toward an integrative definition.

Postscript: Missional Is Wesleyan and Wesleyan Is Missional

It is our hope that as you have worked through Part One of this book you have come to appreciate and share the conviction that Methodism (with its deep roots in Wesleyan thinking and theology) and being 'mission-shaped' belong together in a profound and practical way. That 'mission-shaped Methodism' is virtually a tautology. That, at its best, Methodism is raised up by God to be grace-filled and mission-shaped by the best of both *missio Dei* and Great Commission understandings of mission, and consequently, that evangelism (offering and proclaiming Christ in word and deed) remains intrinsic and essential. Some short statements may be helpful as we turn to offer insights on several biblical passages.

The missional church lives by the grace of God. We understand that God's grace is present in the lives of others before we encounter them, that the grace of the crucified and risen Lord saves us (Ephesians 2: 8-9), and that our growth in grace finds expression in the love of God and neighbor.

The missional church knows that church is not an end in itself. The church exists to bear witness to the love of God in this world. A church's vitality or strength is a by-product of its mission beyond itself—*koinonia* is the result of *missio Dei*. The mission is for the sake of the world, and in this God is glorified (John 17).

We do the mission for the sake of the mission. We cannot control outcomes or even visible fruit. This does not mean that we do not count people, money or other resources. It simply implies that we serve as faithfully as we know how, combining faith, intelligence and rigor, and we trust the end result to God.

The means of grace sustain the missional church. The mission of God is more than a human endeavor or a political activity: it is work that calls forth our love of the neighbor, which cannot be separated from the love of God. In the absence of a disciplined life, in which we are in touch with the means (ordinary channels) of grace, we become disillusioned with God and apathetic toward our neighbor.

Holiness is always personal and social. The missional church holds together (in its own life) the yearning for spirituality and justice. The missional church hears the still small voice (I Kings 19) and the cries of the oppressed (Exodus 3). Personal holiness without social holiness is escapist. Social holiness without personal holiness is works righteousness.

The missional church is connectional. Because we know that the gifts of God are within and beyond our local expressions of fellowship, and because we understand that human needs are greater than our local capacities to meet them, we rejoice in and depend upon our connections with the denomination, our ecumenical partners, friends in agencies, and structures who work for the common good.

The present, broad context requires a missional church. The attractional church is an expensive endeavor that depends on large sums of financial capital and creates consuming participants. The missional church is most at home in the deepest aspirations of people: to be healthy, to be educated, and to be employed. These basic needs were the place of connection in many of the missionary movements in prior generations and are unfortunately growing in our own time.

Young adults resonate with the missional church. Many in the younger generations are seeking a community that has integrity (no hidden agenda), is not hypocritical (separating personal and social holiness), is not judgmental (and thus knows a gracious God), and is real (and thus includes both "winners" and "losers" in our world). They will search for this community, and if necessary, they will piece expressions of it (such as spirituality or justice) together wherever they find it.

The missional church is committed to offering Christ to all, by appropriate words and apt deeds. It is intentional about finding authentic and contemporary ways of inviting people to become lifelong and world-transforming disciples of Jesus Christ.

In summary, the Wesleyan tradition embodies (at its best) the core of what it means to be missional: abundant grace, holiness, discipline, evangelism, an open table, a world parish, and a liberating hope.

Pause...

Which of these various statements is the most significant for your local church at this moment in time? Why?

Offering Christ and Great Awakenings: Past, Present, and Future

The act of "offering Christ" describes a journey that begins with one's own sense of self-awareness that we are created in the image of God and that this is about dignity and rights and potential. All of this is related to what is worthy of being salvaged or saved. Many of us can and do trace a decisive place along the Christian journey to precisely this moment—"my chains fell off, my heart was free."

We readily acknowledge that alongside self-awareness about being created in the image of God is a deep awareness of inadequacy (sinfulness)—a fallen *imago Dei.* Therfore, Christ is offered to save, rescue, or help us—to do what we cannot do for ourselves. Such themes were certainly a significant part of the Second Great Awakening, and we can recognize their contextuality rather than their obsolescence. A reimagined evangelism in service to the *missio Dei* and a broad understanding of the Great Commission (as it arises from all four Gospels) will seek to retrieve and rework what is essential from the past and recognize what is missing and indeed needed in the present.

So how do we reimagine and reappropriate the task of evangelism at present in terms of practice, and of course undergirding that, theology and theory?

Most certainly, this will look vastly different than the model of an exclusive personal evangelism. Ken was deeply formed as a young adult in a model of evangelism that was formulaic and depended on shared cultural norms that one either affirmed or rejected. As was Martyn, and his experience of initial conversion is outlined earlier. As well intended as the training and practice may have been, and to be sure it included time wandering amidst the weeds and the wheat, it included assumptions that have needed to be put aside—some arrogance; some judgmentalism;

some imposed morality, preconceptions about gender, behavior, acceptability, and we could go on.

We believe that there is a present need for a different and deeper practice.

Inner Circles of Vulnerability and Authenticity

It emerges from the sense of who is in my inner circle. Who are the people with whom I can be vulnerable, who allow me to be myself, to be authentic and yet teach me the necessity of living beyond myself in vital connection with others, who maintain a necessary relationship with the larger community? In the deep tradition of Methodism, this is the relation of the class meeting to the world parish.

Wesley's classes and bands arose as potent instruments able to take people from the point of decision of saying yes to the offer of Christ, to increasingly deeper discipleship. What are the instruments that best do that today? Small groups of accountability? Churches that do not always focus on the large and loud, but also offer smaller, safe spaces in which honest sharing and trust can grow and thrive? Most fresh expressions do not seek primarily to be attractive in the normal sense of recent church growth theories, but instead are committed to cherishing and discipling people, being contextual and missional, and being instinctively outwards. Because it is in the engagement with others, often others unlike ourselves—rescuing local congregations from being silos for the like-minded—that these necessary friendships and loyalties arise. True mission and evangelism involves vulnerability and authenticity in safe places. In short, church (particularly mission-shaped church) remains needed as the catalyst for this necessary inner circle where vulnerability and authenticity enables growth in discipleship of Christ to take place.

Deconstructing Evangelism as Many of Us Know It

There will also be a necessary deconstruction of evangelism as many people know, think, and practice it: an evangelism of conformity and in some ways oppression of that which is not life-giving. What follows is either design or despair, both being related to our human need for God that we believe is deeply implanted within us. Mortimer Arias, in his work on the subversive memory of Jesus as an evangelist who announced the reign of God, spoke of the kingdom as encompassing the soul, the mind and the body and thus of evangelism as holistic[37]. The reflections on New Testament passages we shared earlier demonstrates this repeatedly and powerfully. Consequently, the deconstruction of evangelism is often a critique of our having neglected some facet of human wholeness and concurrently God's desire to dwell among us through the incarnation. A constructive theology of grace in response to this need (especially the need for communion and relationship) becomes more difficult when there is failure or brokenness or trauma. This is especially true when the harm has been experienced in or through the church, which is sometimes the case, and is further complicated by persistent inequalities, pandemic, and wars.

A Constructive Theology of Grace

Christianity is not merely life enhancing (like therapy or gym sessions) but is life *transforming* which is to say life-giving (John 10) though not always in the usual senses of western individualism, consumerism and materialism. We imagine that many people are coming to inhabit this reality after an intense experience of isolation, lockdown, and disruption caused by the Covid 19 global pandemic.

A constructive theology of grace is so greatly needed today. We confess, over long and sometimes demanding ministries there have been times when we have forgotten the nature and extent of God's grace, and as a result our ministries, decisions, and our very souls have always been the poorer for it. Then through voices and actions (sometimes surprising voices and actions), events, circumstances, or moments of insight and revelation, we have been confronted once again by God's unquenchable, encompassing, transformative grace. "We forgot your grace," we say humbly in prayer, realizing afresh that in doing so we forgot what God is like!

---

[37] Mortimer Arias, *Announcing the Reign of God* (Academic Renewal Press, 1984).

A constructive theology of grace must be designed to recognize that we don't forget God's grace, its potential, its iconoclasm, and its kingdom orientation, etc., even though in reality the nature of divine grace always challenges us. Hence, we wrap it in formulae. So wild grace, liberating grace, grace which challenges and changes, is a constructive theology of grace for today—at least for us!

From Hierarchy to Equality

This is also the movement from hierarchy to equality, which Paul describes in Philippians 2 as *kenosis*. To say "Jesus is Lord" is the ultimate way of de-centering ourselves and flattening the hierarchy of pride to a grounding in acceptance of a higher power. Physically, this is what happens when we kneel at an altar, and of course, altars occur throughout our lives as we die and rise with Christ.

Therefore . . .

If the first two Great Awakenings were closely related to fear of hell and absolution from sin and guilt, a possible third (or next) awakening relates the story of Jesus to the fundamental human search for dignity through equality—the #MeToo movement, the reparations conversation, the movement for full inclusion among LGBTQIA persons and allies, and the distrust of institutions (even if persons need the goods these bodies provide). A friend noted that each Great Awakening was a response to a part of the gospel. It *was* gospel, but not all of the gospel! Could the Great Commission in service to the *missio Dei* in the present moment be a rediscovery (like treasure hidden in a field) of the gospel that sees dignity and worth in each person, that shatters legacies of slavery and bondage as a necessary consequence of the recovery of the image of God in each person, which fully realized is sanctification?

In posing this question we are not suggesting that other parts of the gospel have ceased to be gospel, but that these elements of gospel goodness and truth is the loud word for today. We wonder if this is how a reconstructed, reimagined evangelism will emerge from the deconstruction of the present moment. And we believe the necessary resources, gifts and challenges are within the depth and breadth of the biblical narrative. In our spiritual blindness or hardness of heart, we had simply missed or ignored a part of the truth. For example, the legacies of human slavery persisted through each of the first two great awakenings, even as there were dissenting voices and prophetic acts of resistance. The scriptures can assist and encourage those congregations who would choose to make this the *leitmotif* of their evangelism today.

We believe that avoidance of this deconstructing then reconstructing work will yield three outcomes: an impoverished understanding of holiness, an ever more marginalized church, and an insistence that the work of liberation is unrelated to the person and work of Christ.

Holiness is more than a conception of the soul being won for some larger purpose. It can be the recognition that the body is a temple of the Holy Spirit (I Corinthians 6), that the Word became flesh (John 1), and that our creation is in the image of a God who chooses to dwell among us, and who is resurrected in bodily form (John 20-21). When the church does not incorporate the cry for human dignity and social justice as essential facets of evangelism, the Holy Spirit of God enables these kingdom characteristics to find a home elsewhere, and often at some distance from the church. This impoverishes the mission and integrity of God's gathered people. The work of liberation is at the heart of the Old Testament (the exodus, deliverance from slavery, passage through the wilderness into the promised land) and the New Testament as Jesus' own identity, life, and teaching were shaped by this narrative and would define his fundamental calling into the world.

And all of this, of course, is good news!

How can this constructive work occur beyond the needed deconstruction that liberates a world that the God of the scriptures imagines, on earth as it is in heaven, where everyone sits under their own vine and fig tree?

We believe it is by themes included repeatedly in these pages, both implicitly and explicitly. It is by congregations of people who love

people, who want to serve others in equal partnership rather than superiority, who want to seek and spread the fruits of the Holy Spirit (love
joy peace, kindness, gentleness etc.). So, openness to the Spirit of God is
key. Who wants to belong to a community of people who experience the
real heights and depths of human experience together, rather than try to
live in a sham protected bubble of "everything is OK here." Who believe
in the supremacy of divine grace. Who continue to seek what it means
to *work, speak, and live for Christ* (as Charles Wesley put it). Who don't
require pathological like-mindedness in order to continue in healthy
fellowship with others, and are not offended by continuing struggles
such as sinfulness. This is the context in which third wave evangelism
(and more particularly the congregations that live it out) will be found,
shaped, and lived.

Pause...

*Talk together about your own reimagined understanding
and practice of evangelism, for your local church and in your
context today.*

If We Knew Then What We Think We Know Now

In this final chapter, we offer some observations and comments arising
from our many years of involvement in the Fresh Expressions (FX) movement. It will be of particular interest to those committing themselves to
fresh expressions of church, greater mission-shapedness, congregational
vitality, and reimagined evangelism, whether locally or for a district or
conference, whether lay or ordained, whether volunteer or paid employee.

The Inclusive and Broad Definition of Fresh Expressions Is a Mixed Blessing

When the FX initiative began in the United Kingdom it was decided not to define too closely what a fresh expression of church is. Any attempts at definitions were deliberately vague because the FX team wanted to affirm and encourage almost whatever was proposed by local churches and groupings. Consequently, many fresh expressions registered on the early FX website 'self-identified' some vastly different ministries, communities, and initiatives from the gentle to the radical. This inclusive approach to fresh expressions largely remains the case, but we note a consequence of this deliberate strategy.

It permits some churches to commit to very minor levels of involvement and interest, while considering their participation sufficient. Some fresh expressions are simply re-titled existing meetings, like an established mid-week study group or a Sunday school renamed 'messy church'. "Yes, we're into fresh expressions," can mean we've rebranded our meeting, now let's just continue as we are. Meaning that the more fundamental, searching, sacrificial but necessary and ultimately satisfying processes of discernment and obedience advocated in this book are not undertaken by all churches. Those involved in the promotion of fresh expressions must be about *both* the affirming of what is *and* urging encouragement and positive challenge to all to try new things, to deepen mission-shapedness as a normal and ongoing part of church life.

Experiencing Fresh Expressions Is Much Better than (Simply) Talking about Them

Visiting different types of fresh expressions is a positive rather than negative experience for most people. The fresh expressions teams being created in more and more districts and conferences know this to be the case. If you or members in your congregation haven't visited a *variety* of fresh expressions, we encourage you to get in touch with those taking a lead in your denomination and make arrangements. Early in Ken's work with fresh expressions, he traveled with a team from Florida to England to visit with twenty-one leaders in the movement over the course of eight days. The team discovered what very many people have found: fresh expressions are very different, that they provide ideas and inspiration, and as such are realized to be attainable. Those who say, "We couldn't do anything like that in our church," often come to see and say that they could and should!

But a word of caution. Care must be taken not to use certain flagship fresh expressions as places to be visited to the extent that they cannot flourish. Plants don't fare well when being constantly pulled up to see how they are growing, and generally speaking, goldfish bowl fresh expressions don't deepen and develop as they likely would without constant visitors. So, if your role involves arranging such visits, bear this in mind and spread visits around!

Appreciating What Fresh Expressions Can't Do and Can Do

It's important to realize what fresh expressions of church are able to do and not do, and to make this clear to those you share with, encourage, lead, teach or mentor. They are not the latest magic bullet, a remedy to our institutional decline and all other ills promising a nostalgic return to a (largely mythical) golden age. Nor is the call to be more mission-shaped the latest management strategy for failing organizations called church, even if some elements of becoming more missional utilize insights and learning from other disciplines and contexts. Nor is being mission-shaped merely attractional church writ large, though many fresh expressions possess very attractive features.

In our experience, however, and repeatedly, mission-shaped churches and fresh expressions do some much needed and quite wonderful things. They very often engender authentic and transformative Christian faith and a deeper discipleship of Christ. At their best, they are living embodiments of Dietrich Bonhoeffer's beautiful concept of "life together under the Word".[38] And for this very reason they exude energy and excitement about God's mission. They reimagine the meaning and experience of both mission and evangelism in that they are primarily about sharing them-

---

[38] Bonhoffer, *Life Together*, 1978.

selves and their life together with others. They are (although this is rarely acknowledged openly even though we have found it to be common in the lives of pastors and congregations alike) an antidote to the boredom of much church life today, and the spiritual depression and malaise brought about by living through a time of continuing long-term decline.

We note an irony here. Much of what lay and ordained church leaders pray fervently for, in terms of a revived and renewed congregation and denomination occurs naturally and regularly when seeking greater mission-shapedness, forming fresh expressions, engaging in church planting, pioneering ministries, and reimagined evangelism. Yet these very things are often untried, unwanted, and rejected by those who desire the renewal they so often bring about. Consequently, effective advocacy of these things is a nuanced and subtle thing. Rarely are people harangued into engaging positively with something they don't think they like or are fearful of. Good advocacy is, then, like fresh expressions themselves, gentle, winsome, invitational, and experiential.

Some Key Principles of Church Growth Theories Remain Helpful and Informative

Church growth theories are often deemed old hat nowadays, though they have evolved hugely since the days of McGavran, Pickett, and Wagner, and we believe still speak usefully into fresh expressions and mission-shaped church thinking and practice. We mention two here:

First, the observation that contextual, cultural, religious, and spiritual factors appear to enable certain groupings and environments to be openly receptive to growth and transformation more than others. Anyone whose role involves working with many congregations knows and experiences this to be the case.

In every area, district, and conference there will be places and environments where the Holy Spirit is already discernibly at work, often in unexpected ways. We have found that, sensitively nurtured and resourced, these places often become fertile fresh expressions. Seeing what God is doing and joining in, is mission 101 after all. "Sensitively nurtured and resourced" is a subtle thing however. We've found that, especially at first, such places need encouragement and occasionally explicit permission to do and be what they feel called to. We've also become aware that offering or providing resource is much more than finance and funding. To be sure, few fresh expressions can exist on thin air, but not all require or desire significant and lasting denominational capital. For example, training those on the ground is in some cases much more valuable resourcing. One fresh expression in London was effectively started when a group of younger women (all unpaid volunteers) moved to do something among homeless people in their area. When asked by their denomination what would help them best, they asked for two things: a modest sum to pay for childcare while they immersed themselves in the initiative and help identifying a training course for them to learn how better to support homeless people living on the streets. A more common offer (the possibility of a paid person to come and lead the group) was dismissed out of hand. Indeed, we've noted that importing a paid person (whether a lay or ordained professional) into contexts where there is already an emerging group or congregation is rarely the best response. Indeed, it does not honor the movement of the Holy Spirit that is already calling forth gifts. In terms of providing or offering resources therefore, local discernment is usually right rather than wrong.

We mention this because as more and more people are employed as cultivators and facilitators of fresh expressions and congregational vitality and so on (which is wonderful) both better and poorer practices are becoming clearer. For example, it is extremely tempting for such post-holders to seek to offer their input equally to dozens, sometimes even hundreds of congregations. It may even be written into their job descriptions. In our experience, Methodists sometimes appear to work as if "equally available and open to all" is defaulted into their sense of vocation. However, this is rarely possible or sensible, particularly over a longer period of time. We can think of many a good worker becoming burnt out, dispirited, and depressed by spreading themselves too thinly, or by trying to get everybody on board before moving forwards. Even more damaging, but not uncommon, are those workers who disproportionally focus on those local churches most resistant to what they are advocating, going the extra, time-consuming and energy-sapping mile to win them round. We suggest seeing where the Spirit is moving is a good criterium for a strategic work pattern. Benign neglect of those people and places seeming impervious to what you are advocating is (at least for an initial period) a proper strategy. Take care, however, to take regular stock of signs of openness and new readiness, because the Spirit of mission works in people's hearts and lives, and congregations evolve and alter. What seems a closed thing at one time may later be fertile.

The next phase of a good work strategy is to begin to allocate time, energy, and appropriate resources into the places where you discern something *can* happen, working with others open to explore just what this might be. In short, we have found that focused rather than blanket approaches to the creation and support of fresh expressions and greater mission-shapedness are more fruitful and sustainable, both for workers and congregations alike.

A second insight from church growth theory that still pertains in relation to fresh expressions and mission-shaped churches is the Homogeneous Unit Principle (HUP). This is the principle that congregations and communities are more likely to grow when they consist mainly of people with certain similarities and commonalities. Early church growth theories suggested that the less cultural or linguistic 'distance' people had to traverse to join a Christian congregation, the easier that journey would be and the greater the number of those who could make it. We make no attempt at a careful evaluation of the HUP here, save to say it has had its critics. Is it a kind of ecclesial apartheid? Is it found in the New Testament? Isn't a Christian congregation open and welcoming to all? And we have theological sympathy with those views. For more than a decade, Ken oversaw a large and diverse Conference which included leaders and communities from many nations. The last church in which Martyn had pastoral charge in the United Kingdom (in central London) had roughly thirty different ethnicities in formal membership in one large congregation. It had its moments, was not always easy, but it was a taste of heaven!

Our support of the HUP in relation to fresh expressions then is not primarily a theological preference for homogeneity but rather a recognition that the principle still appears to hold good in practical terms. Although we like to think all our churches are welcoming and open to all, the reality in most congregations (including the majority of inherited congregations we know) is that they are homogeneous in several significant ways, whether that be ethnicity, color, language, or social class. Likewise, in fresh expressions where the instinct to reach new people—in new places—in new ways means some are formed and shaped deliberately to attract certain interest groups. This was one of the profound insights of the *Mission-Shaped Church* book, namely the emergence of networks. The common factor (an interest in surfing, biking, kayaking, tattooing, recovery from addictions, or shared life experiences) is the unique selling point of that fresh expression, at least at the point of its early formation.

A key learning for those committed to fresh expressions is to work hard to discern what type of expression of church intersects with the real needs and opportunities of an often complex social and cultural context—real, rather than perceived or assumed needs of others. Because, crucially, fresh expressions are created for others having listened carefully to others.

Transform/Evolve What Is Already There

In every District and Conference, a good number of churches will already have many outreach ministries and missions. In some cases, the openness that resulted in such ministries coming about is a continuing openness to further mission-shaped initiatives, such as fresh expressions; this is wonderful and to be encouraged. In other cases however, churches already engaging in several outreach ministries and missions are those which say that they can't engage in fresh expressions or reimagined evangelism because they have no spare capacity, being too busy already doing many good things. Which is understandable and not to be criticized, without abandoning gentle challenges to consider new things. The difficulty of achieving change in such situations should not be underestimated. Repeatedly down the years we have found Methodist meetings far more ready to propose new things to do (often to already exhausted congregations) rather than consider giving up anything that they currently do (which has contributed to the exhaustion). In this way, we avoid the pruning needed in our lives and communities which is at the heart of John 15 and the necessity of this for the fruitfulness promised in the gospel!

Notwithstanding these challenges, the main task is about reimagining ministries with an even greater level of mission-minded intentionality and openness to transformation of what is already being done. So a food bank ministry, a children's after-school club, or even the large day school on the church campus is not abandoned, but is rethought and recast.

A key book published near the beginnings of fresh expressions was Ann Morisy's *Beyond the Good Samaritan*. In it, she argued that good-works ministries by churches were vital but did need to be differentiated from secular local authority projects undertaking the same good things.[39] There needed to be a "value added" element simply because it was an outreach ministry of the Christian church. She was not relegating the value of presence ministry, nor advocating in your face evangelism, but was posing a clear challenge: what is the added value factor of a ministry undertaken by Christ's church?

Our experience suggests that many local churches have responded to the needs of others in stunning ways. We know of churches (small and large) whose commitment to 'missions' is sacrificial and moving. It is very often, however, about raising money to send somewhere. It is often raising money to employ other people to do good works among people, nearby and faraway. Such charitable and philanthropic commitment remains critically important. The value of a greater focus on mission-shapedness and all it entails is that it helps provide the critical value added to established outreach ministries or missions in many inherited churches. The clear fresh expressions emphasis on seeking to make Christian disciples of unchurched people (which is usually different in tone, content, and aim to membership classes in more traditional congregations) is helpful

---

[39] Ann Moirsy, *Beyond the Good Samaritan: Community Ministry and Mission* (Woonsockett: Mowbray Publishing, 1997).

in this context. Also helpful are their instincts about seeking equal partnerships with others, often in neutral meeting places, conscious that some
well-established church outreach projects unwittingly exude impressions
of somewhat arrogant ownership by a benign but zealous landlord. Or
again, their tendency to replace traditional methods of evangelism with
imaginative and contextual ways of offering Christ, within the normal
life and outreach of the fresh expression community, which helps reduce
the common perception of a distant church of a detached deity.

Whether it is well received or not, those advocating mission-shapedness,
fresh expressions, and reimagined evangelism do well to encourage and
help inspire the transformation and evolution of what already is being
done in many inherited churches, as they are able and as a key element of
their work. However challenging it is, such work is not outside their remit,
alongside this and just as important. In many cases it is better and easier
overall to create a new congregation or sub-congregation rather than trying
to change an existing congregation (and in the process, often ruin it).

We've learned, and sometimes sadly forgotten, that fresh expressions
necessarily includes the practice of *church planting*, rather than nagging
existing congregations to become or do something they don't want to—at
least not yet.

Over our long ministries as pastors in Christ's Church, and human
leaders in our small corners of it, we are well aware that the pervasive
drift is to a mindset of managing decline and negotiating conflict. In
recent decades both the United Methodist Church in the United States
and the Methodist Church in Britain have closed many more churches
than they've opened. And, almost inescapably, pastors and leaders find
themselves spending more time and expending more energy in ending church congregations well (so-called hospice ministry) and dealing
with painful fallouts. Therefore, in a sense, urging church planting of
fresh expressions of church seems nonsensical. Yet we should not be
scared of promoting and talking regularly about planting and growing
new churches. The important thing to make crystal clear is that we are
not talking about replicas of a model of church of which there remain
plenty, but rather churches that are different, varied, tuned to need, to

others, and are deliberately contextual and profoundly incarnational. We are convinced that that critical need cannot be met fully by adapting elements of life and ministry in willing inherited churches, important though that is. Crucially there also needs to be fresh expressions blooming like an ecclesial springtime, in a context that more often feels to be the onset of a long winter.

Consequently, all sorts of different Christian people committed and called to a resolute and lasting intentionality to create new church communities of many kinds are much needed. In some senses this entire book is written to help aid such a call. For those holding church leadership roles in these days, there is the clear challenge to engage and change the default mindset and narrative about being a declining church. We are, but that's not the whole story, nor is our decline wholly negative. Increasingly, we belong to a denomination which *both* closes churches (often for good and proper reasons) and plants and grows lots of new ones—though there is still progress to be made. Employ sensitively "turnaround initiatives" adopted by several denominations including the United Methodist Church (but not yet the Methodist Church in Britain)

Sometimes the location and condition of a church building is more mission potent than the congregation who currently inhabit it. There are times when the present (faithful, aging, tired, and declining) congregation needs to end, but without the closure of that church and often sale of the premises that normally accompanies such an ending. Then (often after an appropriate period of closure) strategic input deliberately intended to help create a new congregation is placed there. These are some of the basic themes of turnaround initiatives adopted by increasing numbers of historic denominations around the world. Some church leaders will not use them, and we understand why. It easily feels unpastoral; it's painful. Those who seek to implement turnaround rarely win any popularity contests.

While recognizing these sober realities, we are advocates of sensitively using turnaround processes in the toolkit of urging greater mission-shapedness, throughout Methodism and beyond. Of course, turnaround strategies must be undertaken with care, compassion, understanding, listening, and discernment. But in appropriate circumstances, it must happen. We both know of many successful turnarounds where an existing building strategically useful to the witness and mission of the church has become the home of a new congregation. In all such cases it is important to have a careful and sensitive 'exit' plan and know what the USP of the new congregation is required to be. This comes through careful listening to the context and those who know it, rather than assuming or believing we know what's best for people. And unless things are going clearly wrong, we believe these new congregations must be left to become what they are, without a lot of interference, for no less than several years. If that means some of the normal expectations or responsibilities (excepting those of safe sanctuary and legal requirements, etc.) placed by the Conference on its churches can be waived or suspended for a time, all the better.

Workers: Clergy and Laity

Laity are at the forefront of many local fresh expressions and outreach ministries that are amenable to becoming fresh expressions. Alongside them, but not automatically taking a leading role, is a supportive ordained person—an 'outrider'—sometimes required to protect the fledgling community from the queries and protests of others. Where things are already working well, a strategic leader should think long and hard before assigning a Deacon or Elder to take charge—especially an Elder assigned from elsewhere who doesn't know the neighborhood, context, or people involved. On the contrary, the key role of an Elder or Superintendent is to encourage and enable the right kinds of oversight, support, and resourcing.

We have also come to realize that there are some clergy and laity who can lead fresh expressions (and mission-shaped churches) and some who can't. This is just as in any other specialized ministry. It is not, as some assume, either an alpha or a male role—far from it in fact. In British Methodism, a rigorous selection process was created to identify pioneer ministers who were both lay and ordained. It became clear that not everyone who said they felt called to pioneering ministries of various types could actually do it. Consequently, making wise and careful assignments to fresh expressions is just as crucial as any other context of Christian ministry. This may well require new criteria of selection and evaluation, and new people to oversee these processes of vocational discernment.

There is fast coming down the line (if not already here) the significant issue of clergy training and formation. We are realizing increasingly that those offering for ordained ministry come disproportionately from good, mission-shaped inherited churches and fresh expressions. Our observation is that poor inherited churches are producing fewer and fewer people with a call to ordained ministry.

Consequences of note arise from this realization. Such folk enter, (most) complete training then are often assigned to churches quite unlike those which birthed and nurtured them, and in which they experienced their call to ministry. They become therefore disillusioned. We believe that there need to be specialized programs of clergy training about topics such as mission, ecclesiology, pneumatology, church planting, and pioneering. We are encouraged to see such programs being created and offered, but they largely remain extra, voluntary (and expensive) post-ordination opportunities, rather than a normal key part of initial training for contemporary Christian ministry (as they need increasingly to become). What we need in a trained pastor is changing. Accordingly, those with responsibility for creating curricula or appointing college staff, those serving on the boards of training institutions and Conference selection committees need to be deeply aware of the changing needs of our churches. Otherwise, we are training people for models of ministry that are increasingly disconnected from those which are crucially needed. Being ready for 1977 when it comes round again simply will not do!

When both/and Becomes Either/or

If it's not already arrived, there will soon come a point when fresh expressions and pioneering ministries cease to be "exotic." Some Districts and Conferences (particularly in these heavy days for United Methodism and other denominations) are at that point. Up to now, fresh expressions are regarded as something of an experiment. It is an experiment which may enable the status quo to continue a little longer, staving off more profound decline and change, a negative, reactionary view that readers will not be surprised to know we do not share. In both our Conferences and many others, the cost of fresh expressions initiatives has normally been found from special funds. The result is that neither the wider denomination nor its local churches have yet felt the financial pinch in any meaningful way. It has been largely both/and up to now. We believe this era has ended or ending soon. We are quickly reaching a point when resourcing the creation of fresh expressions and transitioning inherited churches to a contemporary mission-shape that necessarily involves the unthinking and reimagining of evangelism must become normative rather than exotic. The special initiative money is drying up, and we are in an increasingly either/or situation. So hard choices must be made. While the present and future may not seem like a time of abundance of resource, we are confident in God's promise of sufficiency.

This leads to questions. Do we continue to consider normal funding as given very largely to supporting existing systems and patterns of being church? Or do we move progressively to investing in fresh ways of being church from our normal, regular funding streams? Advocates, outriders, and supporters of fresh expressions and mission-shaped churches will be required to contend and urge holy risk-taking in their District and Conference. Rely on the Holy Spirit. She wants this even more than you do!

Appeals and Apologetics in "either/or" Times

What might be the appeals made for fresh expressions and mission-shaped churches in these days? Down the years we have both preached and taught what might loosely be termed the apologetics for these things, mainly but not exclusively to our own Methodist Churches. We outline the main elements of many such appeals here, in note form.

Methodism Has a Profoundly Missionary, Evangelical Ecclesiology

Great care must be taken not to present this statement as, "Methodism is better than other Christian denominations and groupings." It isn't. But, like all Christian denominations and traditions Methodism/Wesleyanism possesses certain tones and emphases within Christian orthodoxy. So, unlike those Christian groupings whose origins lay in persecution and a belief that only believers can legitimately be baptized; or whose origins are about the particular identity and autonomy of a gathered congregation and the nature of its pastoral ministry; or those whose origins are in secession and reformation as defined by Canon law and authorized liturgical texts—the origins of Methodism, coming about later in time and put simply, lies primarily in none of these things. The origin of Methodism lies in a recognition that Christ must be offered to all and is able to be received by all. In consequence the vehicles of belonging (at least at first) are not normal pastor/congregation models. Rather, they are models that enable those who respond positively to Christ offered to them to become devout Christian people. Classes, Bands, and Societies were adopted and amended because they served the primary aim of making disciples of Christ. Methodism, then, has a profoundly missionary, evangelical, and adaptive ecclesiology. It is who we are. And when we are not, or cease to be, we become unlike ourselves and depart from a key reason why God raised us up at all. Fresh expressions, mission-shaped churches, a continuing commitment to find appropriate ways to "offer Christ" to all is in our ecclesial DNA. This is why we believe what we advocate in this book is profoundly Wesleyan and Methodist.

A Belief in the Prevenient Work of the Holy Spirit of God as the Spirit of Mission

The emphasis on God's grace has been a thread running through this book. A common delineating of God's grace into prevenient, saving, and perfecting aspects of grace has been rehearsed. Each of these is emphatic and evident in the nature and life of fresh expressions of church. A more recent evolution of thinking about God's prevenient grace is that it is not only evident when people first become aware of God's nature, call, and purpose for their lives but is also evident in God's mission in the world through the person and work of the Holy Spirit. The Spirit is abroad in the world, working and wooing the things of God upon "Adam's fallen race" as Charles Wesley put it. Our study of scripture passages earlier in this book make clear our urging of our Church to join the Holy Spirit of mission in her active work in every place and context. The kinds of church, community, and people that can best aid and accompany the Spirit is at the heart of our appeal for mission-shaped churches and fresh expressions.

The Catholic Spirit

Methodism, at its best, is committed to the Catholic spirit. John Wesley's famous sermon and later letter to a Roman Catholic focus on Catholic love or a Catholic spirit. A common quote put in modern language is, "If your heart is as my heart is, if you love God and all humankind, I ask no more: give me your hand." Just what the Catholic spirit is and is not is currently a hot potato for Methodists (particularly whether or not specific beliefs are important) closely related to the issue of whether people of contrary convictions can live happily together in one local congregation, or even Conference[40]. Our focus is more upon fresh expressions of church as a fruitful and authentic means of adopting the Catholic spirit. It involves less xenophobia, more acceptance, more partnering and befriending of other Christians (and others) in the work of God's mission, and recognizing the active work of the Holy Spirit in people and places we traditionally might think her not to be present. At their best, fresh expressions are an example of active participation in the Catholic spirit. We have no doubt that the present moment—one of continuing recovery from pandemic and polarization—cries out for this Wesleyan gift, awaiting our rediscovery, like treasure hidden in a field.

Fresh Expressions Are Not New

All through Christian history, the nature of the Church of Jesus Christ has been evolving and adapting. It certainly has its foundations, but in terms of its expressions (both physical and spiritual) it changes and is

---

[40] John Wesley, "A Catholic Spirit," *53 Sermons*, 1771.

plural. It spans from the desert fathers and mothers, monastic orders and their various houses, cathedral builders and Quaker meeting rooms, grand basilicas and humble chapels, and finally circuit riders preaching in the open air under trees. Even today, in some places, small, almost silent Christians meet in small groups in homes, in contexts of social and sometimes physical persecution. Church expressions change and are always various. But because most of us don't live long enough to see the ecclesial paradigm shifts, we don't think they do. As someone put it, "if nobody in a church can remember when something was done differently, it must always have been done this way, mustn't it?" No! Church, including a variety of fresh expressions of church, is normal rather than abnormal Christianity.

Honor Your Forebears in Faith—Hold Fast to the Charisms of Your Founders

All our inherited churches were newly planted at one time or another. We often forget that. The large numbers of them, which today we sometimes wonder what to do with, are evidence of a huge and sacrificial commitment on the part of our Christian forebears to plant and build a church here in this place. Note how often the first church planted was small (in a kitchen, converted home, or barn) and only later a dedicated chapel or church building was built by a growing congregation. The current fresh expressions movement is not the first such movement among Methodists.

The Methodist past is often subject to much romanticism. But the huge resources of Methodism did not come about through faint-heartedness about the gospel or Christ's commission to his Church. Fresh expressions honor the innovative, missional, evangelistic way our forebears in faith pursued so passionately. Let us not misuse or neglect our spiritual or material inheritance. Fresh expressions honor our spiritual ancestors.

Our Church Is Never "Ours"

This is sensitive in a sad time of fragmentation and disaffiliation. But despite the generosity of commitment of church members (often over many years) and the love in which many hold their local church (specifically people and the premises) our churches are never truly ours in the same sense which we might own a company or a house. Our churches always belong to Christ—as we do. We are stewards of them, some of us leaders in them for a season, some of us earning our living through working in and for them, but church is never ours to own or do what we like with. Despite so often being shaped as we like it, the prior call of the Church and each local church is to be faithful and obedient to its Lord. To realize this is to be released to accept and pursue the main themes of this book.

Gatekeeping and Window Opening Blessing Future Generations

With sufficient exceptions to keep us hope-filled, contemporary Methodism in many parts of the world is mainly a community of older people. Our repeated appeal to congregations of older, faithful folk is this: please commit yourselves consistently and persistently to being less gatekeepers of existing church and its resources, and more window openers to change.

When Martyn was president of the Methodist Church in Britain, he visited many parts of the Connexion (that's how it's spelled in Britain). On a visit to Shetland, he stayed with a delightful older couple for several days, which was the setting for a key story recounted many times down the years. We share it here at the conclusion of our book.

Donald and Zena were devout Christians and wonderful hosts. They proudly showed me around some of the main islands of Shetland. They had attended the Methodist church in Lerwick for very many years and shared with me a concern about groups of youths seemingly aimless on the local streets and their idea that a room in the church could be gifted to them to play games or listen to music.

On Saturday afternoon I spoke about fresh expressions in the Lerwick church and mentioned, in response to a question, that the most effective youth ministries I knew of were when a youth worker was appointed to work among young adults, someone quite near their own age, and without a heavy expectation upon them that their task was to get backsides in church on Sundays.

The meeting over, we drove back in virtual silence, and I knew something was wrong. I asked, "Is everything alright, Zena?" It wasn't. She'd heard my response to the question as a criticism of her own desires about a youth space in the church premises and her genuine longing for youngsters to encounter Jesus Christ. "You've said my plans and dreams are wrong" she said. I was mortified and apologized, trying to explain and repair the damage as best I could, and bless her. She softened, but was still unusually quiet.

The rest of the day was filled with meeting local people over a meal, an evening meeting at which I preached, then back to their lovely home and to bed. In the morning over breakfast, the three of us sat round the table, and I witnessed a wonderful conversation between them.

"Donald?"

"Aye."

"We've got four children, haven't we? (A curious question to ask your husband of over 50 years, I thought, and tuned into the conversation.)

"Aye." (With a hint of "Where is this going?")

"And if we could give them, or our grandchildren something that they needed, to help or bless them, we would, wouldn't we?"

"Aye." (With more than a hint of "where is this going?")

"Well, I've been thinking. Our church has meant everything to us. We met there, got married there, the children were baptized there and attended Sunday school there. It's there we came to faith, and I'm so grateful for all that and I love it and all our friends there. Don't you, Donald?

"Aye." (With an active interest in "Where is this going?")

"Well, I've decided. Anything that we can do to ensure that people like our children and grandchildren might come to faith in Jesus and have a loving supportive community like we've enjoyed all these years, we've got to enable that to happen. Even if it means our church changes so we don't like it as much."

They became "window-openers"—people who said "yes" to any idea, project or initiative that increased the prospect of future generations finding Christ and belonging to a community of his people.

Many Donalds and Zenas will never be zealous advocates of fresh expressions. But they can urge and enable their local church and denomination to pursue the means whereby new people in new places in new ways can encounter Christ and find a place among his marvelous people.

Printed in the USA
CPSIA information can be obtained
at www.ICGtesting.com
LVHW041351210124
769165LV00008B/922

9 781953 495884